The Art of Museum Exhibitions

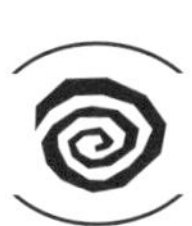

The Art of Museum Exhibitions

How Story and Imagination Create Aesthetic Experiences

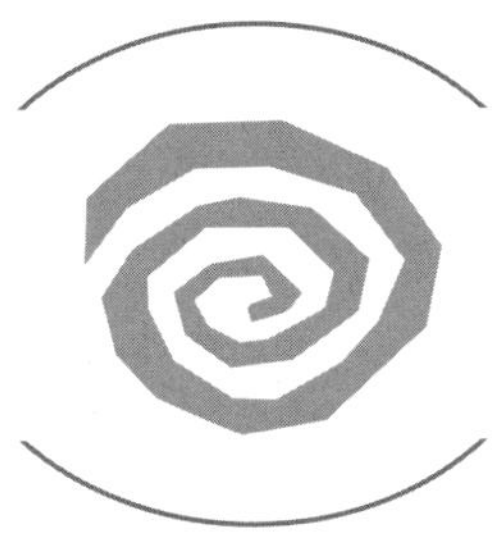

Leslie Bedford

Left Coast Press Inc.

WALNUT CREEK, CALIFORNIA

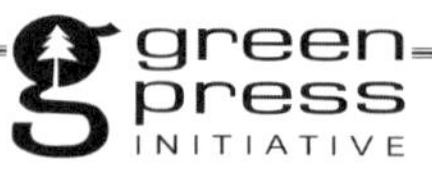

Left Coast Press, Inc. is committed to preserving ancient forests and natural resources. We elected to print this title on 30% post consumer recycled paper, processed chlorine free. As a result, for this printing, we have saved:

2 Trees (40' tall and 6-8" diameter)
1 Million BTUs of Total Energy
169 Pounds of Greenhouse Gases
915 Gallons of Wastewater
62 Pounds of Solid Waste

Left Coast Press, Inc. made this paper choice because our printer, Thomson-Shore, Inc., is a member of Green Press Initiative, a nonprofit program dedicated to supporting authors, publishers, and suppliers in their efforts to reduce their use of fiber obtained from endangered forests.

For more information, visit www.greenpressinitiative.org

Environmental impact estimates were made using the Environmental Defense Paper Calculator. For more information visit: www.papercalculator.org.

LEFT COAST PRESS, INC.
1630 North Main Street, #400
Walnut Creek, CA 94596
http://www.LCoastPress.com

ISBN 978-1-61132-310-8 hardcover
ISBN 978-1-61132-311-5 paperback
ISBN 978-1-61132-312-2 institutional eBook
ISBN 978-1-61132-704-5 consumer eBook

Library of Congress Cataloging-in-Publication Data
Bedford, Leslie.
The art of museum exhibitions : how story and imagination create aesthetic experiences / Leslie Bedford.
pages cm
Summary: "Leslie Bedford, former director of the highly regarded Bank Street College museum leadership program, expands the museum professional's vision of exhibitions beyond the simple goal of transmitting knowledge to the visitor. Her view of exhibitions as interactive, emotional, embodied, imaginative experiences opens a new vista for those designing them. Using examples both from her own work at the Boston Children's Museum and from other institutions around the globe, Bedford offers the museum professional a bold new vision built around narrative, imagination, and aesthetics, merging the work of the educator with that of the artist. It is important reading for all museum professionals"-- Provided by publisher.
Includes bibliographical references and index.
ISBN 978-1-61132-310-8 (hardback) -- ISBN 978-1-61132-311-5 (paperback) -- ISBN 978-1-61132-312-2 (institutional ebook)
1. Museum exhibits--Psychological aspects. 2. Aesthetics. I. Title.
AM7.B353 2014
069'.5--dc23
2014001936

Printed in the United States of America

The paper used in this publication meets the minimum requirements of American National Standard for Information Sciences—Permanence of Paper for Printed Library Materials, ANSI/NISO Z39.48–1992.

Contents

Acknowledgments

As the reader will soon discover, the metaphor for my thesis of exhibition as art form is a tent. Its tent poles are three big ideas drawn from theory and practice: story, imagination, and aesthetic experience. I owe this metaphor to Elaine Heumann Gurian, who encouraged me many years ago to think about making major decisions—for example, should we move from Boston to New York?—by deciding which of the several tent poles—job, marriage, children, lifestyle—came first. I have used the same language over and over in counseling my students and younger colleagues.

The creation of my initial doctoral thesis, the basis for this book, rests as well on several tent poles: those individuals whose wisdom and kindness enabled me to construct my doctoral program and dissertation. I want to thank them publicly:

- My doctoral committee at Union Institute and University: Susan Amussen, Douglas Quin, Jay Rounds, Lila Staples, John Tallmadge, and especially George Hein, a valued friend who has generously advised me over the years;
- Michael Spock, who graciously gave me permission to draw freely from his collection of Philadelphia Stories;
- Dan Spock for the summative evaluation—and many brilliant ideas—of the exhibition, *Open House: What If These Walls Could Talk?* at the Minnesota History Center; and
- Elaine Heumann Gurian, Marjorie Schwarzer, Kieran Egan, Holly Fairbanks, Madeleine Holzer, Tom Hennes, Ken Brecher, Kathleen McLean, Lynn McRainey, Gillian Judson, Darcie Fohrman, James Volkert, Andy Merriell, Jim Sims, Don Hughes, Nancy Haffner, Steve Brosnahan, Fred Ellman, and Jay Featherstone, as well as the dear and talented friends from my early years at the Boston Children's Museum, including especially Signe Hanson, Janet Kamien, and Leslie Swartz.

The process of turning two hundred-plus pages of academic writing into a book for the field was challenging, and necessitated turning to another cherished group of colleagues.

- I am deeply grateful to Ellen Hirzy, my editor, colleague, and friend, who brought her gifts as a writer and years in the museum field to the task. Watching my ideas and voice come to life in her skillful hands was a wonderful experience.
- Ben Garcia read the thesis, marked it up with myriad Post-it notes, and insisted I not shy away from my "manifesto"—and then meticulously reviewed the book manuscript as well. Dan Spock also read the thesis and challenged several ideas, something I hope he will continue to do.
- I freely borrowed inspirational writings and practices from Mark O'Neill, but he bears no responsibility for the conclusions I reached.
- A number of colleagues and friends generously read and commented on sections, and in some cases, the entire manuscript: Marianna Adams, Lauri Halderman, Peter Samis, Sara Wendell Smith, Will Crow, George Hein, Dale Jones, Karleen Gardner, and Shari Werb.
- Other friends and colleagues went to a great deal of trouble to track down images and other details, including Naomi Coquillon, Lauri Halderman, Andy Anway, Eric Mortenson, Steve Brosnahan, Polly McKenna-Cress, and the many former students who responded to postings on the Bank Street College listserv.
- I would neither have gone back to school for a Ph.D. nor written this book if it weren't for the extraordinary adults—both the students and also my colleagues Claudine Brown, Bill Burback, Janet Rassweiler, and Laura Roberts—with whom I enjoyed collaborative teaching and learning during my thirteen years with the Leadership in Museum Education program at Bank Street College.

Finally—though in truth, the first tent pole that I put into the ground—there is my husband, Frank Upham. While his own field couldn't be more removed from exhibitions as aesthetic experience, he gamely read the dissertation, insisted I turn it into a book, and then made sure I did. I dedicate this to him and our glorious and growing family.

A Note about Methodology

Each chapter begins with a personal story drawn from a series of recorded interviews of museum professionals conducted in 1992 at two national museum conferences. These interviews were gathered by Michael Spock, an internationally known museum leader and former director of the Boston Children's Museum, and a team based at the University of Chicago. These Philadelphia Stories—so named because both conferences were held in Philadelphia—are accounts of memorable learning experiences in museums.

All of the stories come from museum professionals, which means there is a distinctive voice, very different from the more typical "visitor voice" (for instance, the data from the evaluations of the exhibition *Open House: If These Walls Could Talk*, also cited at different points in this book). My initial misgivings—how typical can these insights be?—were partially allayed by Jerome Bruner. In *Actual Minds, Possible Worlds* (1986), he cites a comment by William James that the best way to understand religion is to "study the most religious man at his most religious moment," a precedent he adapts to examining the nature of storytelling through the works of the best writers (15). The Spock stories are not about storytelling but about exhibitions, and several of their narrators are masters of exhibition development and design. They can relate the experience of visiting an exhibition with a professional's depth of insight and level of detail. So in addition to heading the individual chapters, several are used to illustrate theory.

Twelve of the stories, those on pages 21,31, 39,44-45,46-47,49,62,65,71, 93,97,108, 110-111, and 143, were previously published by the American Alliance of Museums in Michael Spock, *A Study Guide to Philadelphia Stories: A Collection of Pivotal Museum Memories*. Copyright ©2000 American Association of Museums, www.aam-us.org. (The American Association of Museums was renamed the American Alliance of Museums in 2012.) I am grateful to AAM for their permission.

Finally, and significantly, though titled *The Art of Museum Exhibitions*, this book does not discuss two major kinds of museums, at least in depth: science centers and art museums. I welcome thoughts from colleagues more familiar with these institutions and have benefited already from editorial comments by art museum professionals. But I claim no particular expertise in either arena.

Leslie Bedford

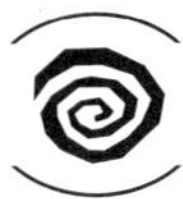

Introduction

My first thirteen years in the museum field were spent at the Boston Children's Museum, a marvelous place to learn the craft. Beginning in the 1960s and 1970s, the museum's major contribution was the clarity with which it put the visitor first. In this laboratory of experiential learning and innovative practice, every aspect of our work—from organizational structure and staff titles to how collections were displayed—was designed to make a difference to our visitors, whether beginning learner or expert, child or adult. Education was the institutional mandate.

The museum had five areas that modeled what our director Michael Spock called "plum pudding," suggesting the rich dessert stuffed with many different kinds of ingredients—in this case, the various resources of the Japan content area.[1] My official title was Senior Developer Curator for the Comprehensive Japan Program Area. This area encompassed a permanent exhibition: an authentic nineteenth-century Kyoto-style townhouse; a sizeable collection housed in a study-storage facility open to the public; programs for families, schools, adults, and experts; a multipurpose space for classrooms and performances; an introductory area for changing exhibitions; and—since staff members were considered resources as well—adjoining and visually accessible offices. At the center stood the visitor.

The museum had no separate education department. Everyone was an educator, and everyone was in the business of education. The classic—and now outmoded—tension between curator and educator didn't exist. I had a master's degree in teaching and had taught in secondary schools for many

Leslie Bedford, "Introduction" in *The Art of Museum Exhibitions: How Story and Imagination Create Aesthetic Experiences*. pp. 11–17.

years, so I understood that people learned in different ways. My approach was essentially constructivist in that I knew instinctively to begin with the familiar before introducing the unfamiliar, but I knew this from practice, not from theory.

Neither today's meaning-making model nor what I had learned as a classroom teacher defined the museum's approach to education. Instead, we chose content based on an intuitive understanding—in later years, increasingly shaped by formal evaluation—of what visitors knew and wanted to learn. We had messages to pass on and employed every technique at our disposal—the more playful and entertaining, the better—to get them across. We were somewhat conversant with Howard Gardner's multiple intelligence theory and bits of Erik Erikson, Jean Piaget, and Lev Vygotsky, and we also acknowledged our debt to John Dewey and the tradition of progressive education—even if few of us had actually read him. The museum was dedicated to learning through doing; education and experience were one.

At the Boston Children's Museum, I had an experience that shaped my beliefs about exhibitions and ultimately sparked the thinking that led to this book. As the senior developer for a major exhibition on international youth culture called *Teen Tokyo*, which opened in April 1992, I became convinced of the centrality of process in developing exhibitions, the existence of explicit strategies that can help visitors inhabit a foreign culture, and the belief in exhibition as a unique medium.

When I left the museum two years later, the staff threw me a goodbye party. One guest, referring to the work I had done in creating *Teen Tokyo*, volunteered to the assembled group that the museum was losing "an artist." I was flattered, of course, and also brought up short. I didn't know what he meant. But the comment stuck with me, not because it made me happy (though it did), but because it puzzled me. Was I an artist? Was the exhibit art? I would never have thought to use that term when describing my work. My brother is an artist; I, on the other hand, worked with a team of people to make exhibitions for families with clear cognitive and experiential goals in mind. In the case of *Teen Tokyo*, I hoped visitors would feel some empathy with the Japanese, understand how small the world was becoming, and experience elements of what people in the field of cultural exhibits call "same but different." These were the goals of an educator, not an artist.

Building a New Vocabulary for Exhibitions

Through the years, I have reflected on the common threads of art and aesthetic experiences and learning in museums, especially through exhibitions. I have considered personally memorable exhibitions: *Mining the Museum* at the Maryland Historical Society (1992); an exhibition on jellyfish at the Monterey Bay Aquarium (1993); the permanent exhibition about John F. Kennedy's life, assassination, and legacy at the Sixth Floor Museum in Dallas; a series of visually and conceptually innovative exhibitions at the Museum of African Art in New York City; the use of object theater presentations at the Minnesota History Center and elsewhere;[2] *Field to Factory: Afro-American Migration, 1915–1940* at the Smithsonian's National Museum of American History (1987–2006); memorials like Maya Lin's Vietnam Veterans' Memorial in Washington, D.C., or the Irish Hunger Memorial in lower Manhattan; and finally my own work, a traveling exhibition for Facing History and Ourselves called *Choosing to Participate*, created in 1998 and still traveling today.

These exhibitions are benchmarks for the medium's potential to transform how visitors understand a particular set of ideas, themselves, and the world. They also share elements that provide a shape and structure—a metaphorical tent—for the exhibition as an artistic and educational medium: *narrative*, *imagination*, and *aesthetic education*.

The first pole that supports this new tent is story—or, as scholars call it, *narrative*. My interest in narrative came from life-changing firsthand stories told by rescuers of Holocaust victims, heard at a teachers' workshop I attended, and later from reading Jerome Bruner's *Acts of Meaning* (1990). Given the foundational nature of narrative, it began to seem that storytelling was the obvious way to engage people in the kind of internal conversation that I believed had to occur for an exhibit to even begin to matter to the visitor. I first tested this idea in 1996 at the Brooklyn Historical Society in a small exhibition about the Brooklyn Dodgers' 1955 World Series win, in which we told the story of Jackie Robinson in terms appropriate for 8- to 12-year-olds. A few years later, I had the opportunity to create *Choosing to Participate*, a large traveling exhibition based on powerful stories from recent American history. I began to talk and write about the kind of internal conversation stories can generate in the listener's mind.

I discovered another tent pole—*imagination*—in the late 1990s when I joined the faculty at Bank Street College of Education and participated in a seminar with Maxine Greene, the distinguished scholar of aesthetic education. In the course of her extraordinary stream-of-consciousness talk, I realized that the process I'd labeled *internal conversation* was really the imagination at work. It was like meeting an old but forgotten friend. Soon, under the tutelage of Kieran Egan, a Canadian scholar who founded the Imaginative Education Research Group (IERG), I learned that the concept of imagination had a history, a developmental component, and possible strategies for putting it to work. And learning about the imagination meant exploring somatic experience or embodied cognition and inevitably new thinking about the mind-body connection.

At about the same time, I read George Hein's *Learning in the Museum* (1998), one of the handful of scholarly and at the same time genuinely useful books in the museum field. As it had for other practitioners, Hein's work gave me the theoretical constructs for understanding what had been instinctive but unexamined practice for many years. We had known that trying to make exhibits visitor focused was right; now, through constructivist theory, we knew why.

Hein is among several thinkers in the field of museum studies who provided further theoretical foundations—supplemental tent poles—for my emerging theory of exhibitions. They include Lisa Roberts, Mihaly Csikszentmihalyi, John Falk and Lynn Dierking, Lois Silverman, Jay Rounds, Nelson Graburn, Kathleen McLean, and many others. Key ideas—that learning is only one way to understand the experience, that each visitor is unique, that wonder and resonance are valid goals, that exhibitions exist within a particular kind of institutional environment, that people visit museums for many reasons, and so forth—sharpened and enriched my understanding and generated still more tent poles for an increasingly expansive tent.

Working in the Subjunctive Mood

As I explored aesthetic education in greater depth in workshops at the Lincoln Center Institute, I learned that each performing art has a unique language. I began to wonder if exhibitions also have a language that helps us understand them as medium. Perhaps, I thought, we could see exhibitions as art form, the visitor's experience as aesthetic, and the exhibition maker as a kind of artist after all. I had come full circle since my first glimmer of a notion that there may be a different model for exhibitions—but the circle had, of course, grown in size.

Along the way, I began to study Spanish and, like many English speakers, found the subjunctive mood intriguing but challenging. We don't often use phrases like "if I were" in English. In any case, the term *subjunctive mood* became my shorthand for imagination, for feelings, for the "what if?" way of thinking that characterizes the arts and seemed to work for exhibitions as well.

The notion of working in the subjunctive mood,[3] and the ever-evolving shape of my metaphorical tent, led me to the central thesis of this book: The creation of effective exhibitions, exhibitions that are true to their unique medium, asks museum professionals to contemplate different goals and evaluation standards. It means working in the mood of "what if?"—the mood of the imagination. This can be the mood of the educator; it is certainly the mood of the artist. And while this approach employs a wide range of tools and habits of mind common to both, it does not support one well-established assumption: that the primary purpose of exhibitions is education, that is, the transmission of knowledge. Rather, exhibitions as a medium are a kind of art form, though not in the classic meaning of the term—Art with a capital A—but as the experiential, imaginative expansion of meaning that aesthetic experience can inspire.[4]

As a medium, exhibitions are both education and art. They exist along a continuum—actually, along several continuums, depending on the lens we use. We can think about exhibitions from numerous perspectives—as identity work or as social work, as participatory experience or as opportunity for civic engagement, and as education or as free-choice learning. My lens is imagination and how it works through story and the arts. For me, the most effective exhibitions are aesthetic experiences; it goes without saying that they also embody learning, personal identity, therapeutic value, and so forth.

But such a perspective doesn't inform practice, which continues to favor a narrower view. On some deep, if not always articulated level, we hold on to the transmission model of communication that so many thoughtful people have worked to deconstruct. We think—or at least act as if we think—that we are in control, that the museum can determine the visitor experience. My commitment to exploring exhibitions as art form thus springs not from a wish to turn the clock back to exhibitions as elitist exercises in contemplation—the usual and not infrequently maligned way of thinking about aesthetics—but rather from a firm belief that they are interactive, emotional, embodied, imaginative experiences.

About This Book

How can we reframe the conversation and see exhibitions more as art than as education? In the following chapters, I will explore this question—deconstruct my tent—drawing on both theory and practice, which must be in constant conversation. It is critical to examine the *why* and not leap immediately, as we often do, to the *how* and the *what* of our work. Part 1, Contemporary Exhibition Theories, reviews the thinking of leading contributors to current models. Chapter 1 examines the premise of exhibition as education and how museum history, museum education, and visitor studies have shaped today's understanding of the medium. Chapter 2 introduces alternative voices from anthropology, social work, design, and elsewhere that collectively uncover the complex pattern of ideas currently beginning to animate our work.

In Part 2, Constructing a New Model, I move on from these more familiar voices to introduce scholars and ideas less commonly considered in the museum field. Three chapters review three "tent poles" that are fundamental to my thinking: narrative, imagination (including imaginative education and embodied imagination), and John Dewey and aesthetic education.

In Part 3, Working in the Subjunctive Mood, I consider what this new model looks like in practice for those who work with objects, text, design, and interpretation. What habits of mind should every member of an exhibition team, regardless of task, adopt in order to create an aesthetic experience for visitors? This chapter works on the assumption that the what-if language of the imagination is the appropriate one for a medium that is imagined or constructed by both maker and visitor and thus is not about transmitting knowledge but creating meaning.

Working in the subjunctive mood means working with the imagination, opening minds to alternative ways of thinking and being—seeing things as other than they are. Imagination is the catalyst for thinking and learning. We let go of entrenched beliefs about what constitutes art, and begin to see the aesthetic qualities of exhibitions that create memories and meaning for many visitors. For the particular medium of exhibitions, the integration of imagination with aesthetic experience is especially appropriate. The language of the arts can also be the language of exhibitions: objects rich in meaning; stories that evoke emotions such as empathy; metaphorical play to forge new connections; design that melds space, light, image in one integrated experience. An aesthetic approach can capture and inspire the deepest kind of personal meaning making, with its potential for transformation. And, finally, to work well, it requires the highest standards of practice; it asks exhibition makers to work more like artists, not simply translators of knowledge. I think my generous friend from the Boston Children's Museum was correct: all of us on the *Teen Tokyo* exhibition team were artists. Just as the aesthetic experience encompasses both the art and the visitor, it includes the maker as well. They form a whole—if the experience is to be, in John Dewey's words, *an* experience.

PART ONE

Contemporary Exhibition Theories

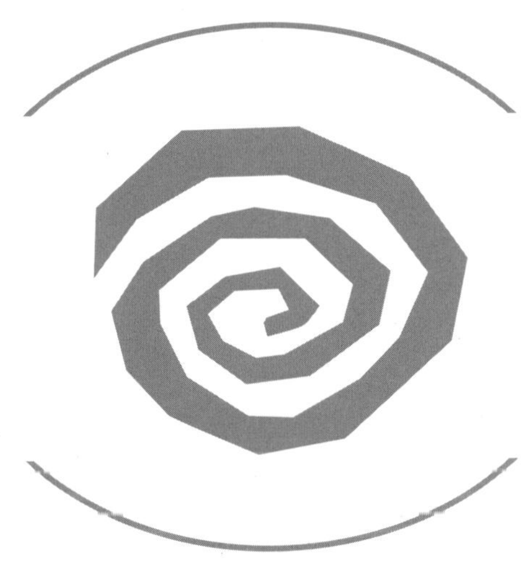

Chapter 1

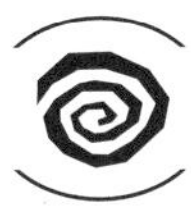

Exhibitions as Education

I know that when I was a kid, something in the [American] Museum of Natural History in New York made a big impression on me, but I didn't know that until I was an adult. Because I found myself, in my early twenties, around the time I was interested in working in museums, visiting the Museum of Natural History.

I was studying anthropology, so I took a walk through the anthropology halls, and I turned this corner and there was this moment, this shock to me, of something that was a very deeply buried image from my childhood that I had never thought about, this image just came back to me with a shock. And it was seeing a diorama of a South American Indian hunter . . . It was a full-size mannequin, and he had a blowgun in his hand, and he was aiming it up at this little patch of trees and forest with birds in it, in a very dark hall, with a light on him.

And, as I came upon this in my twenties, it was like some door suddenly opened, and I realized that I had suddenly seen this when I was a child. And there was just this recognition of something that was very strange, powerful, a little scary, and also just fascinating. What was this all about? . . . I don't have any more intellectual content to put to that, but it was something that had obviously made a deep impression, was buried all those years, and I never knew about until I discovered it again (M. Spock 1992, 16.3; 2000b, 21).[1]

Leslie Bedford, "Exhibitions as Education" in *The Art of Museum Exhibitions: How Story and Imagination Create Aesthetic Experiences*. pp. 21–38.

Since first opening to the public, museums have been educational institutions. As Alma Wittlin wrote in 1949, "the creation of the Public Museum was an expression of the eighteenth-century spirit of enlightenment which generated enthusiasm for equality of opportunity in learning" (quoted in Hein 2006b, 2).[2] But for and by whom and according to which principles and what practices such education was to be achieved was contentious, and remains so. George Hein (2006b) provides a thorough review of our current understanding of the evolution of both the educational mission of museums and the scope of work and professional training required for those who implement it. For the purposes of this book, the most important point is the emergence and continuing prominence of museum education as a separate field and function in the twentieth century. But regardless of who was in charge of the work—director, curator, docent, or educator—or how broadly or narrowly defined, museums and exhibitions, their most public medium, were and are designed to educate.

This chapter explores some of the rich stew of current thinking about exhibition as an educational medium from three perspectives: museum history; the well-established but still-evolving field of museum education (with a brief note on design); and the relatively new area of visitor studies. An analysis of the exhibition *Choosing to Participate* illustrates the practical implementation of many of these ideas while highlighting the inevitable tensions between theory and practice. In chapter 2, this palette of ideas expands into other domains, including social work, anthropology, and participatory design, with the goal of unpacking the traditional model of exhibition as education—one still enshrined in practice in many, if not most, museums.

Museum History

In *Museums and American Intellectual Life 1876–1926* (1998), historian Steven Conn calls museums "sites of intellectual and cultural debate where the prevailing cultural ideas and assumptions of American society were put on display and where changes in those assumptions were reflected" (12–13). His analysis of how and among whom this debate transpired during the formative years of the modern American museum provides a critical foundation for understanding contemporary thinking about museums and exhibitions.

These nineteenth-century institutions—art, natural history, anthropology, and history museums—embodied the Victorian worldview, what Conn calls a "metanarrative of evolutionary progress." As he says of that time, "a trip through the galleries followed a trajectory from simple to complex, from savage to civilized, from ancient to modern" (1998, 5).

At the heart of this optimistic narrative of progress were the museum's collections, the artifacts supporting the era's "object-based epistemology," and the important role museums played in creating and disseminating knowledge. According to Conn, objects "were seen by many intellectuals as yielding new knowledge and museums, not universities, were seen as the places where the work of producing that knowledge would take place" (1998, 15). Knowledge was inherent in objects; visitors did not require additional interpretation since they, like curators, were assumed to be able to read the record inscribed within the objects.[3]

Conn does not discuss museum education—which assumes an interest in the visitor—perhaps because it didn't really exist. While the mission of nineteenth-century museums was fundamentally educational, neither the role of educator nor an articulated philosophy of teaching and learning were part of the original landscape. But as Hein has pointed out, at that time, the world of formal education had an equally impoverished understanding of both public access and pedagogy (2006b, 3). By the late nineteenth to early twentieth centuries, however, differing perspectives on the core mission of education were becoming identified with leaders in the field. George Brown Goode at the Smithsonian Institution argued for educational programming but drew the line at schoolchildren; Benjamin Ives Gilman at the Museum of Fine Arts, Boston, became known for his advocacy of the aesthetic experience but paid attention as well to the nonconnoisseur; and John Cotton Dana established the Newark Museum with the goal of social and civic utility (Hein 2006b, 4–5). These perspectives continue to play out today.[4]

But it wasn't until the late twentieth century that "the visitor experience"—as a formal term and a field of inquiry—came into its own. In the meantime, it seems unlikely that the typical practitioner would have questioned either the evolutionary metanarrative or the established understanding of how learning happens. Knowledge existed independently of the learner and thus could be transmitted intact through collections and, starting in the early 1900s, through programs, labels, and trained docents.

In truth, museums, like anything else, are products of their times. To celebrate its 2006 centennial, the American Association of Museums commissioned

Marjorie Schwarzer to write the lively and thorough narrative *Riches, Rivals, and Radicals: 100 Years of Museums in America*. In an earlier draft of her chapter on exhibitions, Schwarzer reviews the influence of contemporary trends in thought on the ways museums created their exhibitions:

> In the 1920s, museums looked to the Cyclorama and world's fairs. The goal was realistic environments for collections, like habitat dioramas and period rooms. From the 1930s to the 1950s, they looked to the Bauhaus and new fields like industrial design and photojournalism to invent the white cube. The goal was neutral environments that ordered the world according to textbook precision. During the 1960s and '70s, they looked to educational psychology and political activism to design active learning spaces. The goal was connection and social relevance. In the 1980s and '90s, they looked to multiculturalism, computer technology, and business team models. The goal was multi-sensory environments that could convey multiple points of view (Schwarzer 2004).

Aside from Schwarzer's book and a handful of other writings, little has been published about the history of museums' interactions with their visitors. For the most part, the field relies on the writings of thoughtful practitioners who tend to focus on the present rather than the past. A good example is Gail Anderson's *Reinventing the Museum,* an edited collection of articles illustrating her widely shared theory of change in twentieth-century museums, which she labels the "paradigm shift" from collection-driven to visitor-centered institutions (2012). Anderson also cites and summarizes other changes in her "Reinventing the Museum Tool," a table comparing traditional to reinvented museums according to their institutional values, governance, management strategies, and communication ideology—some fifty-two pairings in all. For instance, she says that compared to a traditional museum, a reinvented institution believes in civic engagement and multiple viewpoints, is mission driven and models shared leadership, is a learning organization committed to strategic positioning, and welcomes differences and dialogue. She encourages institutions to use these terms as part of an internal dialogue and self-assessment. The late Stephen Weil, a lawyer, deputy museum director, and intellectual spokesman for the field, summed up the reinvented museum most succinctly in the title of his contribution to the *Daedalus* issue on America's museums (1999): "From

Being *about* Something to Being *for* Somebody: The Ongoing Transformation of the American Museum."

While I subscribe to and teach this perspective, I share a concern that we adopt it too literally. Museum studies is a new field (aside from a handful of nontraditional schools, there is as yet no doctoral program in museum studies or museum education in the United States), and we have too few thinkers to guide us. Lacking strong grounding in history, we too easily fall for what Gary Kulik calls the evolving morality play of the development of the modern museum: from "aristocratic patronage and fear of vulgar crowds" to public funding and the "embrace of all" (Kulik 1992, 11). The division between traditional and reinvented, among other issues, underplays the ways in which nineteenthth-century museums emphasized public education.

Nevertheless, Anderson's paradigm shift is useful and frequently invoked, and certainly the concept of visitor-centered practice has gained enormous currency in recent decades. Regardless of when the transformation actually began and how widespread it is, the notion of a shift represents a view of museums that contrasts in many ways with the nineteenth-century model that Conn and others have detailed. And it has enormous implications for the theory and practice of exhibitions.

Museum Education

Although museum history and institutional context provide useful insights into understanding exhibitions, another set of theoretical frameworks looks more explicitly at the medium itself. These models come from the fields of museum education (rather recently rearticulated as museum or free-choice learning) and visitor studies. While many museum educators and exhibition staff may never have studied the history of museums, they are likely to be familiar with the work, or at least the names, of those scholars whose ideas have enriched the conversation about exhibitions. This chapter looks at three examples: educator and scholar Lisa Roberts's focus on interpretation as narrative; George Hein's approach to constructivist educational theory; and John Falk and Lynn Dierking's work in visitor studies. Other highly influential thinkers include Howard Gardner and his theory of multiple intelligences;[5] Mihaly Csikszentmihalyi's work on flow and the meaning of objects (see chapter 5);[6] and the writings of many other scholars and practitioners whose work continues to enrich the field.[7]

Lisa Roberts and Postmodernism

Lisa Roberts, who trained as a museum educator and became a museum director, analyzes challenges to the nineteenth-century canon in *From Knowledge to Narrative: Educators and the Changing Museum* (1997).[8] She focuses on the presumption that exhibitions should display a body of expert knowledge acquired through scholarly research and transmitted intact to all visitors through the curator's selection of objects and text, with some limited assistance from a designer. Drawing on the methodologies of ethnography (participant observer on the exhibition team) and literary criticism (exhibition as text), she uses the development of an actual exhibition from the Chicago Botanic Garden to explore several critical themes in museum education: education as entertainment, as experience, as empowerment, and as ethics. In her final chapter, "Education as Narrative," she summarizes where the field is now and some of the implications of this ongoing evolution. Her goal throughout is to highlight the major role educators have played in effecting and institutionalizing this change.

Within her extensive discussion of the history of entertainment vs. scholarship, Roberts refers to the recent field of leisure studies to support the thesis that museums are a form of leisure activity for which an understanding of visitor motivation is critical.[9] This emerging perspective argues that exhibitions need to be enjoyable, possibly playful, and even fun. Her focus on the needs of the visitor resonates with the emerging impact of postmodernist thinking on the museum field, which, for the most part, has been slow to appreciate its import.

The term *postmodern* refers to the mid- to late twentieth-century seismic epistemological shift that challenged the premises of Enlightenment-modernist thought—for example, the existence of absolute truths and the supremacy of reason as the basis of knowledge. The newer relativistic perspective of postmodernism posits the importance of sociocultural and other contexts for understanding how each individual, through personal interpretation, creates his or her own meaning; there is no truth to which all would subscribe, and reason becomes only one path for self-discovery.

Postmodern thinking thus challenges the very raison d'être of museums: their authoritative interpretation of the objects in their collections, the foundation of the museological canon. The new scholarship claims that what matters isn't what the museum owns or displays but how the visitor interprets it. Personal experience becomes as legitimate a source of meaning as curatorial knowledge, which, according to this point of view, is also contextual and interpretive rather than unassailable truth. In Roberts's view, with the advent of postmodernism, "the very nature of museums' exhibit function has been altered. Once a seemingly straightforward matter of displaying collections, exhibition can be viewed as an eminently interpretive endeavor: not just that the information exhibits present is subject to multiple interpretations, but the very act of presentation is fundamentally interpretive" (Roberts 1997, 74–75).

The new focus on individual interpretation converged with changing notions of authenticity, of what constitutes the "real," and thus of what exhibitions are about. If exhibitions are acts of personal interpretation that need to be entertaining as well as educational, then how can one define and include the authentic object (see chapter 6)?

As the field's growing understanding of how people actually interact with exhibitions began to shape both approach and content, the medium was reframed as participatory experience, a new model that could best be crafted by someone versed in the new understanding. That person was not the curator, who would be too wedded to content expertise, or the educator, who might only care about communication, but a new, hybrid agent: the exhibition developer.

Pioneered at the Boston Children's Museum in the late 1960s and 1970s, the role of exhibition developer has become standard practice at children's museums, science centers, and several exhibition design firms. Most museums, however, continue to rely on curators—who are unlikely to be trained in educational theory—to organize exhibitions. A curator may work closely with or at a distance from educators, evaluators, and designers, or professionals from these three groups may be brought in near the end of the process to design programs and turn the curator's ideas into a three-dimensional experience. The central role and authority of an exhibition developer thus represents a significant change in practice, reflecting a major shift in thinking about what and for whom an exhibition is created. These changes continue to be discussed in the field today.[10]

Roberts sums up where these developments have taken museum education: "The essence of the education enterprise is thus the making of meaning" (1997, 133). She cites cognitive psychologist Jerome Bruner, who postulates two basic modes of thought: the paradigmatic or logico-scientific mode, which would support the transmission model of education (Steven Conn's object-based epistemology is part of that tradition), and the narrative mode, which involves the creation of story. For Roberts, Bruner's narrative mode offers an apt and applicable description of learning in museums. Essentially, it provides a big conceptual and methodological umbrella under which all the converging changes in the field can be identified and negotiated. In Roberts's view,

> narrative provides a useful "narrative," if you will, for describing the nature of education in museums. It accommodates the various meaning-making activities engaged by curators and visitors as they interpret and order the world; it provides the terms under which different versions may be true; and it comprises the means for judging and evaluating those versions. If education is a process of assessing different worlds, narrative is the means by which this is accomplished. Consequently, our ideas about both "learning" and "teaching" must be reformulated (1997, 136–37).

Roberts's work is a convincing analysis of the state of the field in the late 1990s and how it got there. But two areas—the tenets of constructivist educational theory and the role of the exhibition designer—deserve further elaboration.

George Hein and Constructivism

George Hein's *Learning in the Museum* (1998) provides a foundation in learning theory—including the thinking and practice of the great twentieth-century philosopher John Dewey—that complements Roberts's work. While Roberts traces the historical development of narrative or meaning making through literary theory, Hein incorporates the new paradigm within the educational philosophy of constructivism, including its practical applications. He thus restores Dewey to his rightful place as the grandfather of modern museum education (Hein 2004, 2006a). Not only did Dewey best articulate the tenets of education as the learner's experience and active construction of meaning, but his progressive education model provided the philosophical bedrock for the first visitor-centered exhibitions developed at the Boston Children's Museum and San Francisco's Exploratorium in the 1960s and 1970s.

Hein argues that constructivism is the educational theory best suited to museums. The epistemological foundation for constructivist theory and practice is the belief that all knowledge is constructed by the learner personally or socially rather than existing outside the learner. Constructivism insists on the active nature of the learner's mind; learning is not the incremental absorption of knowledge by an essentially passive mind, but the active and ongoing construction and transformation of knowledge by an individual.[11] Therefore, a constructivist approach to teaching, including through the medium of exhibitions, requires employing different strategies for different learners; recognizing the importance of prior knowledge; reinforcing conceptual access through, for instance, the display of familiar objects; and respecting the standard of developmentally appropriate practice. Above all, constructivism supports and enshrines multiple interpretations; there is no single right answer.

The terms *constructivism* and *meaning making* are often used interchangeably in the museum field, undoubtedly because they appeared in the literature at roughly the same time. But one refers to a specific educational theory and the other to a naturally occurring human activity (see Hein 1999; Rounds 1999). They share a contextual, learner-centered, process-oriented perspective on practice. Constructivism would be more likely to refer to creating knowledge and meaning making to creating understanding. Thus, Roberts, from the perspective of literary theory and the humanities, and Hein, with his foundation in educational theory and evaluation, helped lay the theoretical grounding for today's exhibition-as-education model, which in turn dovetails with and implements the wider paradigm shift to the visitor-centered museum.

Roberts's and Hein's books were published in the 1990s. More have been published since, some of which are discussed in chapter 2. Worth noting here is the broadened mandate and expanded self-confidence that museum education enjoys. Education is at the center of the museum's mission, and museum educators, whose professional training and status have only increased in recent decades, are more apt than before to be found at senior levels and working across the institution. In fact, among more progressive institutions, distributed leadership and a cross-departmental team approach have supplanted the more conventional top-down, hierarchical, and silo-bound methods of old. Along with this shift have come new definitions of museum education, more commonly called learning (see "Visitor Studies" later in this chapter).[12]

Design

Although design typically is not part of a museum educator's professional role, Hein and many others embrace its importance in crafting educative experiences. (The differences between an exhibition—let alone a simple brochure—that was professionally designed versus one crafted by an aesthetically challenged content or audience advocate are enormous.) Current trends in design, in particular "participatory design," will be addressed in chapter 2 and later in chapter 6. In earlier days, exhibition designers, like educators, were brought in after an exhibition's content was fixed, and their job was to try to make it work visually and spatially. In the newer world of meaning making, however (with or without constructivist theory and practice), the designer plays an enhanced and more critical role, institutionalized in part through the series of professional development institutes funded by the Kellogg Foundation in the 1980s. Held at Chicago's Field Museum, these sessions focused on the team approach to exhibition development and encouraged the field to incorporate design perspectives from the beginning of the process rather than waiting until the ideas, typically called the exhibition script, were all laid out. In other words, the designer became another voice in the process of interpretation. In recent years, we have witnessed the growth of courses and graduate programs in exhibition design.

Visitor Studies

Another player, the evaluator, soon joined the ideal exhibition team, thus ensuring that visitors' perspectives would influence the design through ongoing evaluation.[13] This enterprise is called visitor studies.[14] One of the most prolific contributors to visitor studies research is the husband-and-wife team of John Falk and Lynn Dierking, founders of the Institute for Learning Innovation (1986–2012). Since the National Science Foundation, an early advocate and funder of exhibition research and evaluation, funded much of their work, their earlier findings in particular tended to focus on science centers. Their books—in particular, *The Museum Experience* (1992) and *Learning from Museums: Visitor Experiences and the Making of Meaning* (2000)—are required reading in many graduate programs.

Pulling together a variety of findings (many of them their own) and disciplines, including human development, education, psychology, and neuroscience, Falk and Dierking encourage a view of museums as institutions of free-choice learning that can best be understood through a "contextual model of learning." By *free-choice*—a term they have championed so successfully that it appears to have completely usurped the earlier *informal learning*—they mean nonlinear, personally motivated learning that involves considerable choice on the part of the learner. It operates within a set of overlapping and interdependent contexts—the personal, the sociocultural, and the physical—through the prism of experience over time. In their terms, "learning can be viewed as the never-ending integration and interaction of these three contexts over time in order to make meaning" (Falk and Dierking 2000, 11).

This issue of time is intriguing and important because it challenges established evaluation practice. How is one to evaluate the impact of a program or an exhibition if the visitor may not even be aware of what she learned until many weeks, months, or even years after the encounter? Falk and others have increasingly called for more longitudinal studies, and Michael Spock's *Philadelphia Stories* (1992) by museum professionals is an example. The following account speaks vividly to learning over time and how an experience in childhood, when recalled in the right setting, can provide a transformative learning experience:

> I grew up in the Bay Area in California and remember really clearly playing with a particular exhibit at the Lawrence Hall of Science that had ramps on hinges so that they would alternatively be bridges or valleys, and bridges and valleys, and bridges and valleys. And this machine would go up and down. And you could control the rate at which the bridges would turn into valleys, and there would be balls rolling around. And the point that I thought was always of it was to get the right rate, so it just got faster and faster and faster and faster and faster. But I just loved letting the ball run around and trying to see what I could do with it. And I liked watching it and listening to it.
>
> And I put it out of my mind for about twenty years, until I was in a physics class and found out what a cyclotron was. And all of a sudden I realized that I had a model, a real visceral physical model, of what a cyclotron did, and what each of these electromagnets did to the part—to the charged particles floating around. And each of these little valleys was like the magnet accelerating it down hill all the time, and it gave me a way to understand a cyclotron. And I don't think any other way could have. And it struck me as being important that this had stayed in my memory for more than twenty years. Just because I thought it was fun to make this ball try to go fast. So that's my memory. I must have been ten or eleven years old when I did that (M. Spock 1992, 6–7: 15–16; 1999b, 5; 2000b, 21).[15]

Falk and Dierking are only two of a great many people looking into the nature of learning in museums. Their commitment to publishing accessible books on the subject gives them unique standing; the considerable body of research that shows up, for instance, in issues of *Curator: The Museum Journal* tends to be much narrower in focus and academic in style. It can be difficult for practitioners to obtain and apply the research findings to their work. In addition, most research has been conducted in science museums, in large part because of funding sources but also because, as Jessica Luke and Karen Knutson argue in their article about art museum learning, education has always been central to the mission of modern science museums, often called science centers (2010). The other types of museums—art, natural history, history—have been around much longer and are more apt to fall within the "traditional" rather than the "reinvented" paradigm (see Anderson 2011).

Regardless of discipline, however, there are several stumbling blocks to arriving at a clear idea of how people learn in museums. The major one is definitional: What do we mean by learning? Getting at the answer requires establishing a theoretical framework to organize the research. For example, is learning primarily individual and personal, or is it social, something that happens through interaction with others, whether fellow visitors or museum staff? Is it mostly cognitive, aesthetic, or affective? Can it be construed as stages of development along a novice-to-expert continuum? And how is it demonstrated?

More recently, efforts have been made to synthesize research reports for the field. In 2010, *Curator* published a special issue on the report of the National Research Council's Board on Science Education, *Learning Science in Informal Environments: People, Places, and Pursuits.* Some museum professionals praised the report as evidence of a growing recognition of the importance of out-of-school learning. One of its goals was to "broaden the definition of 'learning' beyond those aspects typically considered in formal education, enabling the field to define success on its own terms that are more appropriate to the setting" (Ucko 2010, 131).

Two companion pieces in the issue discuss the report from the perspectives of art and history museums, with Luke and Knutson's article on art museums suggesting some interesting ways in which the two fields could share definitions and methods while lamenting the lack of either an appropriate in-depth analysis or a consensus on the "intrinsic value of art experiences" (2010, 236). This point of view recalls an earlier, quite comprehensive study by Jessica

J. Luke and Marianna Adams, then staff members at the Institute for Learning Innovation, who analyzed decades of research into learning in art museums. Among their several contributions is the identification of four kinds of interrelated and nonhierarchical outcomes or learning dimensions: learning about content, learning about ourselves, learning how to engage, and learning how to learn (Luke and Adams 2008, 6).

Falk and Dierking's *The Museum Experience Revisited* (2012) is an updated, comprehensive, and compelling review of the past twenty years of research into the nature of the multifaceted interaction between museums and their public. The contextual model remains the conceptual glue, they say, but it now encompasses more recent research into visitor identity and motivation and has been applied to a greatly expanded understanding of the entirety of the museum experience or gestalt—from the moment one decides to visit, for various reasons, through every aspect of the time spent in the museum, to subsequent memories and impressions. In fact, Falk and Dierking maintain that these often-powerful museum memories constitute learning: that is, the iterative and deeply personal process of making meaning and shaping it into memory and knowledge. Finally, in a chapter entitled "The Twenty-First-Century Museum," they challenge the field to embrace "radically new models of doing business that optimize personalized and community-based learning, broadly defined" (Falk and Dierking 2012, 298).

Falk, Dierking, and many others from the field of visitor studies have made enormously important contributions to the field. First, they show that people *do* learn in museums. And in the process, they have helped broaden and enrich our understanding of what that learning looks like. There may still be museum staff—especially those in management positions without backgrounds in education or visitor studies—who insist that visitors can and will emerge from their institutions with their minds well stocked with information presented in the exhibitions and programs. But they would be hard pressed to find such a narrow perspective supported by the extensive literature in visitor studies.

Choosing to Participate: An Example of Exhibition as Education

Choosing to Participate (*CTP*), an exhibition sponsored by the educational organization Facing History and Ourselves, is part of a multifaceted national initiative about the meaning of democracy and the role of an individual citizen. It opened at the Boston Public Library in 1999 and since then has traveled to several North American cities. Facing History and Ourselves wanted *CTP* to support its mission of helping "students with a wide range of abilities and learning styles understand that their choices and actions matter, and that young people can, and should, be agents of change . . . in order to promote the development of a more humane and informed citizenry."[16]

In line with this mission, secondary school students and their teachers are the primary audience for *CTP*. As they developed the ideas and approaches, exhibition team members worked closely with Facing History and Ourselves staff, including a teacher advisory board that ensured the approach would speak to young people and reinforce the lessons of the organization's existing curriculum. In addition, a teacher's guide was developed for pre- and post-visits, and a summative evaluation protocol was subsequently designed and distributed to classroom groups. Student groups visited the exhibition accompanied by their teachers, and volunteer guides selected by Facing History and Ourselves led the groups through the experience. At the same time, the secondary audience—the general public—is also important, and the team worked to create an experience that was effective for individuals or groups who were unaccompanied by guides.

Visitors to the exhibition can explore any of its four sections at will.[17] Three sections feature stories drawn from American history. One, from the mid-1950s, is the story of Jesus Colon, a black Puerto Rican man riding a late-night New York City subway, who had to decide whether to offer help to a white American mother and her children. The second narrative describes the ways different groups in the community responded to the integration of Central High School in Little Rock, Arkansas, in 1957. The third story captures the moment when citizens in Billings, Montana, came together to combat a series of hate crimes in 1993.

An orientation section, the "Crowd Scene," invites visitors to figure out "What's going on here?" They peer into a round canvas structure to view a changing photomontage of iconic urban street scenes—a homeless man, a lost child, a couple fighting. They hear the voices of passersby whose phrases—"I'm sorry, I'm in a hurry"—might echo their own everyday interior monologues. The point is to encourage visitors to begin seeing that these ordinary experiences relate to the historical events they will encounter in the exhibition.

The exhibition is a multimedia experience; each section depends on computer-generated video, lighting, and music to enhance the storylines. Designers used the object-theater approach in several places to give visitors the feeling that they are part of the story.

The design team included three professional roles: an exhibition developer, whose job was to work with the client organization on content, including writing text, and take responsibility for exhibition development from start to finish; an exhibition designer with responsibility for turning concepts into three-dimensional experiences, who was also part of the process from the beginning; and a multimedia firm, which developed the various technological components.[18]

The exhibition's design reflects a core theme: We can step outside our familiar circle of obligation and engage with others. Each section is designed as a circle; the one housing the bystander's area is closed, but those in the other three sections open up to enable visitors to explore the stories of people who chose to move beyond bystander to participant status.

For example, one enters the Little Rock narrative along a short hallway lined with photographs and text that relate the history of segregation up to the day when the Little Rock Nine, young people selected to challenge Governor Orville Faubus's defiance of federal law, attempted to integrate Central High School. The visitor finds herself in a facsimile of a teenage girl's bedroom. On the wall hangs a freshly ironed shirtwaist dress; on the bureau, a radio plays period rock-and-roll that is soon interrupted by a motherly voice calling, "Hurry up, Elizabeth. It's time to go to school." Moving through this computer-generated sound-and-light piece, the visitor encounters a giant photo mural of Central High School, which, accompanied by a rising chorus of angry voices, dissolves into an iconic image from this period: African American teenager Elizabeth Eckford, wearing her new dress, schoolbooks clutched to her chest, is chased from the schoolyard by a mob of white people, their faces contorted with hatred and rage. The decision to use Elizabeth's story to anchor the section was deliberate; the design team wanted adolescent visitors, the main audience, to empathize with her as a peer experiencing the universal event of the first day at a new school.

Finally, the circle opens up fully to reveal five areas in which one can learn about the diverse ways that various groups in Little Rock responded to the events of 1957: the Little Rock Nine, white students, parents, community leaders, and politicians. The exhibition ends with "Connections," a place for visitors to sit, reflect, and—if so moved—add their own personal stories about choices they have made in their lives.

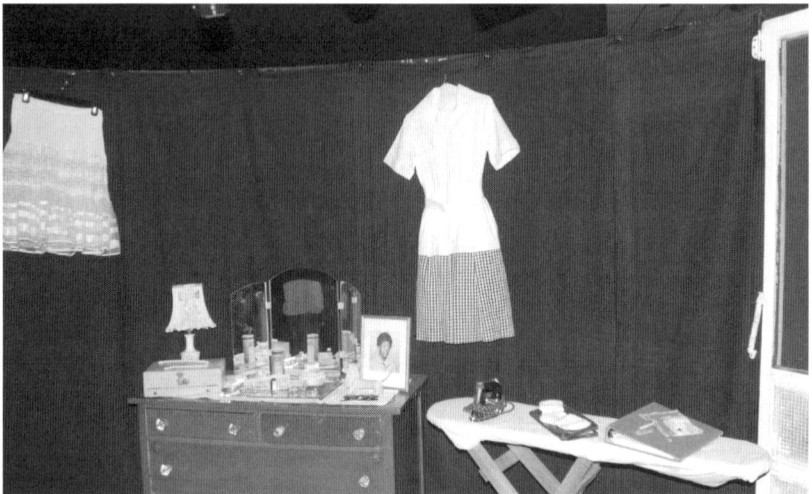

The "Crisis in Little Rock" section of *Choosing to Participate* included an imagined mock up of Elizabeth Eckford's bedroom including a copy of the shirtwaist dress she wore the day she attempted to enter Central High School. Photo courtesy of RBH Multimedia, Inc.

CTP illustrates how aspects of the contemporary version of the education model can play out in an actual exhibition. It is about narrative—stories, not objects. Apart from some iconic photographs, the most memorable object, Elizabeth Eckford's dress, was not the real thing but a copy made from photographs. In line with the early ideas of Kathleen McLean, Beverly Serrell, and other experts, the exhibition does have a core idea that the team wanted visitors to take away from the experience. But this message—"my choices make a difference"—asked visitors to construct their own meaning, their own narrative, and to experience the journey in affective as well as cognitive terms. In line with today's museums' willingness to advocate social policy and create exhibitions that transform visitors' thinking and perhaps even their behavior, the ultimate and undeniably reformist goal of *CTP* is to inspire civic engagement. Employing formative evaluation techniques, learning theory, and specific references to the visitors' own lives, the design team, lead by a developer instead of a curator, sought to be as visitor-centered as possible. The design reinforced the content while providing random access; there was no pre-set pathway through the experience. And finally, it opened not in a museum, but a public library.

Despite the many ways in which this exhibition differs from education in a classroom, it is and was always understood to be an educational enterprise. While knowledge, at least on a theoretical level, may have been reframed as personal, contextual interpretation—as narrative—by the design team, it is still knowledge: the exhibition exists to teach visitors what Facing History and Ourselves thinks they need to learn. In placing the focus on the personal experience of each learner, the educational goals encompass meaning making (the personal response to these different, quite emotional stories), constructivism (drawing on prior, often personal experience in reflecting on the stories in order to understand the meaning of democracy), and gaining new information. For instance, Facing History cared first and foremost about teaching secondary school students about the civic and personal importance of these episodes. They trained volunteers to lead groups of students through the exhibition and make sure major content was not overlooked. So sorting out the often-conflicting goals and designing appropriate exhibition strategies was challenging, but ultimately, in the eyes of the team, organization, and visitors, very successful.[19] But when, as is often the case, exhibitions are also required to demonstrate quantifiable outcomes, typically related to school standards, the tensions inherent in the educational model become especially visible.

Conclusion

The challenges of defining the visitor experience in terms of quantifiable learning are huge, as any current museum educator or leader would attest. While scholars like those discussed in this chapter push a more expansive set of measurements—longitudinal, for example—the typical practitioner is more likely to be grappling with the institution's or the funding source's requirements to justify visitors' experience in immediate quantitative outcomes. At the very least, the expectation is that visitors are learning what we, the design team and the institution, have put out there on the floor. There are many reasons, but one must be the continuing influence of the origins of museum education.

Early museum educators were often former teachers, so formal instruction provided the template for education in museums. But over the years, museum learning and visitor studies, reinforced by scholars like Roberts and others, have converged to give museum education a new definition genuinely independent of formal education. With this evolution has come an explosion of research and—despite the heavy hand of school standards and other criteria—a growing confidence in museum education as a legitimate domain.[20]

Nonetheless, the tension between theory and practice remains, as a visit to any institution, large or small, will attest. Stepping back again to view the broader institutional context for exhibitions, it is important to note that despite the narrative of institutional progress implicit in Gail Anderson's book, museums have no more evolved in a straight line than have the exhibitions that they house. Multiple models reflecting multiple understandings often coexist, sometimes within the same institution. And a visit to the galleries of small museums and historical societies can remind us how slowly change comes and how far actual practice can be from the visitor-centered principles that many leading thinkers espouse. What one too frequently finds is a display—essentially, a bunch of stuff to look at—done with scant attention to design and even less to the novice learner.[21]

Such efforts betray the default mode of someone unfamiliar with contemporary ideas about exhibition making. While their creator—typically, though not inevitably, a curator—may be an expert in her academic discipline, she is less likely to be familiar with the fields of visitor studies, informal learning, or design. So to some extent, she has unwittingly borrowed from the nineteenth-century worldview Conn describes: the belief that objects are the key to knowledge, that they can be read by viewers without additional aids, and, more fundamentally, that learning comes through the transmission of expert knowledge rather than through the active engagement of the learner—the constructivist approach. The reasons this approach to exhibitions still exists are multiple and complex. But the fact that it does, even within institutions with exemplary educational programs, only reminds us that institutional context is not all and that change comes slowly and piecemeal.

CHAPTER 2

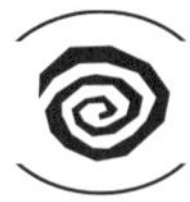

Alternative Exhibition Models

> [This] happened about ten years ago when I visited Dublin. I thought, well, I'll go look at the Book of Kells. I'm not interested in medieval manuscripts, I'm not interested in medieval history, I'm not especially interested in medieval Christianity, but it's a great object and I should go look at it. And I walked up to the case in which it is displayed, and all the hair on the back of my neck stood up and I started to cry. Which was highly unexpected. But I think it was because of the hundreds of years of meaning human beings had invested into the object. And that [was] communicated without any intellectual mediation: I didn't think about it. It was a visceral response to the object itself, which I knew almost nothing about. All I knew was that it was old and it was beautiful, and enormous amounts of time had gone into every tiny little square inch of it (M. Spock 1992, 59–03).

In 1977, the *Journal of Museum Education* published a short and sensible piece by anthropologist Nelson H. Graburn called "The Museum and the Visitor Experience." Graburn argues that museums, like other cultural institutions, must understand and satisfy three kinds of human experiential needs: the associational, which is "an excuse or focus for a social occasion"; the educational, where one learns "something about the world"; and the reverential, which "designates the visitor's need for a personal experience with something higher, more sacred, and out-of-the-ordinary than home and work are able to supply" (Graburn 1984, 180). This framework offers a useful way of thinking about recent, alternative perspectives on exhibitions.

Leslie Bedford, "Alternative Exhibition Models" in *The Art of Museum Exhibitions: How Story and Imagination Create Aesthetic Experiences*. pp. 39-53.

The educational focus, as noted in chapter 1, has a long and continuing history. But interest in the associational, or social, and the reverential dimensions is more recent. The scholars and thinkers discussed in this chapter take a different approach than the prevalent view of exhibition as education. I believe they challenge the fundamental assumption that, as Eilean Hooper-Greenhill puts it, "knowledge is now well understood as the commodity that museums offer" (1992, 2). They are all part of a rich, increasingly complex, and continuous tapestry of thinking about this field.

Theory and practice traditionally have focused on the individual museum experience, but today learning is seen as socially and culturally constructed, and looking at how visitors interact with each other is a critical part of understanding what is going on. In the final chapter of *From Knowledge to Narrative* (1997), Lisa Roberts describes the field's limited understanding of museum learning and proposes a new take on visitor purposes and experiences that encompasses not just education, but also "social interaction, reminiscence, fantasy, personal involvement, and restoration" (138). Several other researchers cited in chapter 1 use a sociocultural lens in examining museum learning and experience. This perspective has profound implications for the field, including staff training and exhibition and program design, because it requires us to examine how visitors interact with each other and the wider world, not simply analyze individual "transformation."

By contrast, Graburn's "reverential" category is about a solitary experience of "contemplation, meditation, and rest from the cares of the world." Recognizing this as a long-established role for museums, some would argue that they disproportionately cater to the needs of reverential visitors, contributing to the public's perception that museums are elitist, intimidating, and basically not for them.[1]

But it is more complicated than that. Reverential museum experiences are deeply emotional ones. And while it may seem obvious that a medium such as an exhibition would speak to the affective as well as the cognitive, the field has been slow to acknowledge it. In addition—and for multiple reasons, including the implementation of the Native American Graves Protection and Repatriation Act (NAGPRA)[2]—many museums have changed their policies regarding the exhibition and care of sacred objects, signaling a shift toward greater respect for indigenous knowledge and the appropriateness of spiritual practices within the museum.[3]

The Social Dimension of Exhibitions

Lois Silverman and Social Work

Lois Silverman is a creative scholar whose work highlights the associational or social-cultural perspective of the museum in original ways.[4] Her doctoral work was in communication, and she has done more than anyone else to popularize the term *meaning making* as key to the visitor experience. From Lisa Roberts' perspective, Silverman's meaning-making model simply expands on what learning actually looks like within such settings as museums. But Silverman is not primarily an educator—her model draws on communication rather than educational theory—and she is after something else. Early in her career, she published a piece on the therapeutic potential of exhibitions called "Johnny Showed Us the Butterflies: The Museum as a Family Therapy Tool." Her research has looked particularly at the visitor experience in history and art museums, as opposed to the science centers that scholars like John Falk and Lynn Dierking have favored.

Silverman finds parallels between the curatorial focus on transmitting knowledge and the early communication theorists' focus on transmitting information. "According to the information perspective, any process of communication involves the transmission of messages or information from a sender to a receiver, through a particular medium," she writes (2002, 5). But researchers began to challenge this model in the 1980s. What they discovered was evidence of a phenomenon far more complex than the simple transmission and reception of intended messages; they discovered meaning.

Silverman offers four definitions of the term *meaning* as they can be applied to the museum experience:

- the communicator's intention;
- a particular understanding of something, *i.e.*, an interpretation on the part of the visitor;
- an individual's subjective valuing of something, *i.e.*, the reason that something is personally meaningful; and
- meaning as "deep, pivotal, memorable, life-changing significance" coming from "those moments of insight, transformation and deep significance—that help us to see the purpose and reasons for living" (Silverman 2002, 5).

The fourth definition of meaning is the one that Silverman wants museums to pay attention to—what she calls the "magic" of the museum, those moments of "enchantment that transpire when people interact with things" (2002, 7).

In 2010, after completing a master's degree in social work, Silverman published *The Social Work of Museums*, a book on the intersection of museums and social service that provides a new and overtly activist lens for examining the museum visitor and experience. Museums, she maintains, have always been about human relationships, which is also the core of social work:

> Thus we begin to see that by making meaning of objects, people in museums are actually developing—and sometimes even changing—meanings and aspects of themselves, their relationships, and the society in which they live. In other words, meaning-making in museums yields beneficial consequences, rendered more concrete through the perspectives of human needs, outcomes and changes, relationship benefits and social capital, social change, and culture change" (Silverman 2010, 16).

But museums need to do much more. They should adopt the categories and needs-based thinking of social workers to help "foster cultures of caring" (Silverman 2010, 139). Such practice, Silverman reminds us, harkens back to John Cotton Dana's Newark Museum during the Progressive Era and is already realized in a variety of museums around the globe.

Nina Simon and Participatory Design

Nowhere has the social dimension of museum exhibitions received more practical attention than in the work of Nina Simon, whose book, *The Participatory Museum,* was co-written with her readers and published online. Simon's blog *Museum 2.0* continues the conversation and often stimulates lively online exchanges.[5]

As Simon cogently explains, the interactivity of the Internet and social media provide a marvelous model for thinking about exhibitions. The museum can be viewed as a content platform rather than provider, opening up the possibility for ceaselessly evolving new ideas and exchanges with other users/visitors. This insight leads Simon to wonder—given what research has taught us about visitors' unflagging interest in themselves and their increasing preference for self-generated content, individual choice, and personal impact—how museums can continue to provide the same old static experiences. As the director of a small art and history museum in northern California, Simon is making her institution a workshop for participatory design. The first question the staff asks itself in evaluating a new idea is, "How can visitors help?" One result is a blurred line between exhibition and program. These two elements grow together as visitors contribute objects, research, ideas, and design. At one point Simon finds herself questioning the value of exhibitions, since programs and events not only drive attendance but reflect what she calls our more "event-driven society."[6]

Simon has opened our eyes to the phenomenon of participation that is already animating every aspect of contemporary life, including the arts: sound artist Phil Kline's *Unsilent Night*, in which participants carry boomboxes to walk and play music together; the interactive theater piece *Sleep No More;* and the interactive art of the Flux Foundation, whose mission is building community through art. These are recent reminders of the power and popularity of participatory experience. The implications of this participatory model for changing practice are enormous: new definitions of authority, a new creative process with new roles, and a greatly changed final product.[7]

Some spin-offs of the participation model resemble the Post-it note talkback boards installed in places like the Boston Children's Museum many decades ago—they solicit but don't respond to input. But others go the next step and let visitor preferences continuously shape the results and thus restore what Simon calls the "broken feedback loop" the field has ignored for so long (Simon 2011, 4). In other words, participants' involvement continuously alters the music, play, sculpture, or exhibition, as happens with, for example, Wikipedia, Flickr, or *American Idol*. In many respects, art museums are leading the way. Some of their new practices, such as the 2007 reinstallation of the permanent galleries at the Detroit Institute of the Arts, in many respects resemble the visitor-centered methods of children's museums and science centers.[8] But others—the use of crowdsourcing to create exhibitions, for instance—are new and exciting. The potential result is a recasting of Stephen Weil's assertion: today's museums are not *about* something or even *for* somebody but *with* us all.[9]

Jay Rounds and Identity Work

Anthropologist and museologist Jay Rounds is the kind of thinker who, as one colleague remarked, "constantly resets our clocks."[10] He asks the field to acknowledge and accept the ways most visitors actually behave in museums, as opposed to how we wish they would: They browse exhibitions driven by simple curiosity, rather than striving to absorb what the museum wants them to learn. The orderliness of the museum helps visitors "create order in consciousness," something Rounds says we need as part of our search for "ontological security." Visitors aren't there to be educated so much as to do "identity work." Museums, he maintains, provide "a perfect setting for public performances of identity. It is a space designed for the display and performance of meaning" (Rounds 2006, 142). We try on a role, an identity, so to speak, and receive validation for it. And while we are unlikely to become transformed by our visits, we nonetheless find opportunities to safely explore alternative identities and thus learn more deeply about ourselves:

> In sum, the museum offers the visitor a whole smorgasbord of exotic ways of perceiving the world, and of living in the world. Museum experiences allow us to flirt with alternative ways of being without undermining our faith with our declared identity. In reality, though, our promiscuous browsing through the museum's riches allows us to explore the possibility that we might become interested in things that are not consistent with our current identity, or that couldn't be predicted from our life trajectory so far. It allows us the guilty pleasures of vicariously living someone else's exotic life for a moment, and to find out how it feels, and how we respond. And all that helps keep open the possibility that someday we might become someone new and unexpected (Rounds 2006, 146–47).

The following example from the Philadelphia Stories illustrates exhibition visits as experiences in "identity work." The speaker, a young woman, talks about walking through *Field to Factory: Afro-American Migration, 1915–1940*, a well-known exhibition in the 1980s about the history of black migration from the fields of the South to the factories of the North. In order to travel from one area to the next, the visitor had to enter a railroad station:

> Well, the most memorable museum experience I have ever had is when I went to the Smithsonian, at the National Museum of American History. And in the *Field to Factory* exhibit there was a sign—there was a station to this exhibit where there was a "white" door and a "colored" door. And I stood there for the longest time not knowing which door to walk into.

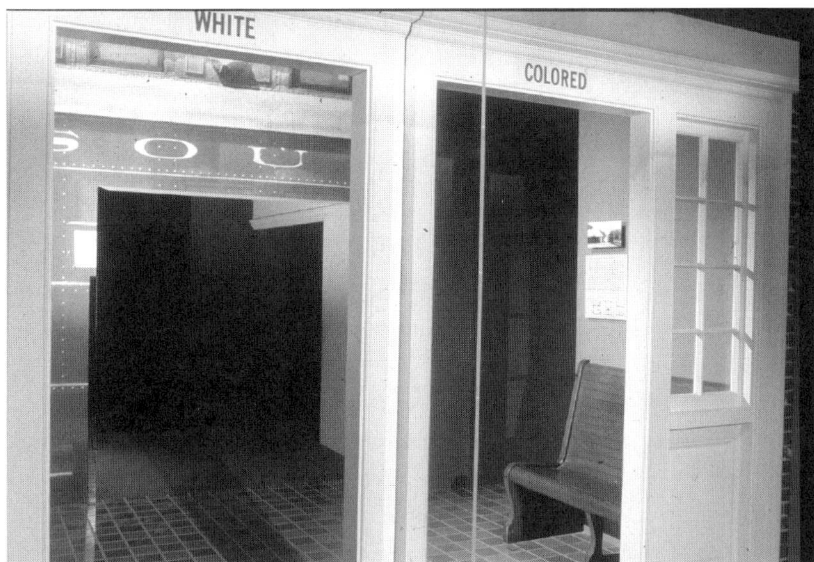

In order to move from one of the *Field to Factory* exhibition (National Museum of American History) to the other, visitors had to decide if they would enter the door marked "Colored" or the one marked "White." Smithsonian Institution Archives Image # 89-3890.

> And it was effective. I mean, that was something that stopped me in my tracks. I mean, I was born and raised, and always considered myself, an African-American, but for the first time I actually thought about my white ancestry that was so far back in generations. And it just kind of stopped me in my tracks. But then I went ahead and I walked in the "colored" door. I figured I had to go with what I knew. And that's the experience that—I mean I will always remember that, because it was something so simple and yet so very, very effective for me as an African-American (M. Spock 1992, 3.23–4; 1999b, 3; 2000b, 19).

Rounds is not the only person to talk about museums and social identity. The previously discussed work by John Falk and Lynn Dierking, *The Museum Experience Revisited,* elaborates on Falk's belief that museums can predict and plan for successful visitation by better understanding how identity-related motivations influence visitors. He describes five identity-related categories—explorers, facilitators, professional/hobbyists, experience seekers, and rechargers—as far more useful predictors of behavior than the classic marketing categories based on demographic data. Not surprisingly, a range of institutions have adopted this taxonomy.

The Reverential Dimension

Stephen Greenblatt's Resonance and Wonder

Stephen Greenblatt's "Resonance and Wonder" (1991), published in the seminal collection of writings *Exhibiting Cultures: The Poetics and Politics of Museum Display,* is one of my favorite essays.[11] Greenblatt analyzes literature as a historicist, that is, someone who seeks to understand things within their historical, geographical, or cultural context rather than according to universal, immutable laws. His essay is an attempt to think in a similar way about art objects and historic sites, "to restore the tangibility, the openness, the permeability of boundaries that enabled the objects to come into being in the first place" (1991, 43). He proposes two models, one that focuses on resonance and one on wonder.

Resonance, he writes, speaks to "the power of the displayed object to reach out beyond its formal boundaries to a larger world, to evoke in the viewer the complex, dynamic cultural forces from which it has emerged and for which it may be taken by a viewer to stand" (Greenblatt 1991, 42). Wonder, on the other hand, is "the power of the displayed object to stop the viewer in his or her tracks, to convey an arresting sense of uniqueness, to evoke an exalted attention" (Greenblatt 1991, 42).

The classic example of wonder would be an experience with a masterpiece, as is recalled in one of the Philadelphia Stories:

> When I was fourteen my father took us on the Grand Tour. He had decided [that for] his version of the Grand Tour we would go to Europe and see the great art museums of the world. So that was the first time I had ever been to see things I had seen in books and had adored. But I had no idea of the scale of them, because a book is—they are whatever they are. And I remember walking into the Uffizi and seeing the Botticelli *Venus*, which was my absolute favorite picture. I mean, if you are a fourteen-year-old girl there is nothing more romantic than the Botticelli *Venus*, unless it's the Botticelli *Seasons*.

> Well, in the Uffizi they face each other in a corner. They look at each other, and they are gigantic. And I nearly fainted, physically fainted, and was so overwhelmed by not only that I was seeing friends I had only seen as little, but that they were huge and that they were gorgeous. And that they were facing each other, so that the entire environment was me and the Botticellis. I had a physical experience then I have never had again in any other place—not in a museum, not anywhere—where I was completely overcome.
>
> And whether I had to sit down or did sit down or had to hold onto the wall I don't know, but it had that quality of losing ground. And it is the landmark experience of all art experiences. It has never happened again. I go to museums all the time because now they are my friends. But this moment where the thing I had seen this size in bad and grainy reproductions, and bad color, was much more beautiful than I had ever imagined. It was all—it was way beyond any fantasy I had ever had (M. Spock 1992, 3.5–6; 2000b, 17).

Experiences of wonder aren't limited to art museums, as anyone who has visited a dinosaur hall with young children can attest. Resonance also can happen anywhere, though objects from the past are most likely to engender what Greenblatt calls "precariousness"—a sense of the fragility of culture and the passage of time—which provides a rich source of resonance (Greenblatt 1991, 43). Objects with resonance have the power to conjure voices long lost in time. Not only single artifacts but entire exhibitions can evoke resonance. In this passage, the speaker recalls her childhood visits to New York's American Museum of Natural History:

> The whole West Coast of the Indians . . . [at the American Museum of Natural History] is exactly the same as it was when I was a child. I've probably been in it a hundred million times . . . Someday they're going to change it because it's so badly done. The lighting is wrong. The explanations are awful. But as a child there, I retained some of that.
>
> The mysticism of that room was just overwhelming. The totems and the sense of wonder and the amazing sculptures; and the sense that trees are that large and they had been somehow carved. It spoke very directly to me as a child. I loved that room. . . . I don't know if I

> learned anything about the Indians, but [it] certainly opened for me a certain sense of communal feeling . . . with people who were very different from myself, that I wanted desperately, at some point in my life, to go back and see, which I have (M. Spock 1992, 14.10–1; 2000c, 6).

Kiersten Latham and Numinous Objects

Kiersten Latham, who writes extensively about how objects shape the museum experience,[12] has interests that fall squarely within Graburn's reverential category. She wants to understand the what and the why of those moments of intensely emotional, almost spiritual and transformative encounters with numinous—from the religious term *numen*—objects.[13] Her past shorthand for such experiences is the "Lincoln hat phenomenon," referring to reports that some visitors to a Smithsonian traveling exhibition began to weep in front of President Lincoln's stovepipe hat.

Latham's analysis of the numinous experience references John Dewey's and Mihaly Csikszentmihalyi's thinking about the nature of an aesthetic experience, especially how such "moments of transcendence, empathy, and awe or reverence" are not limited to encounters with art (Latham 2007).

To learn more about the impact of numinous objects, she interviewed eighteen self-selected visitors to five museums who agreed to talk about times when an object had virtually stopped them in their tracks. Her initial results, published in an article for *Visitor Studies*, looks at the four main themes that characterized the phenomenon of numinous experiences with museum objects:

- *Unity of the Moment:* A holistic experience pulled everything—emotions, intellect, sense of identity—together.
- *Object Link:* The object brought the experience to life and became "a kind of receptacle, holding meaning far deeper and more profound than its simple function or features."
- *Being Transported:* Participants felt they were alone in the moment and often aware of changes in their physical beings.
- *Connections Bigger Than Self:* This sensation recalls Greenblatt's resonance in the sense of understanding one's relationship with others and the greater world, including feelings of reverence, spirituality, and connections with "higher things" (2013a, 8–11).

The Philadelphia Stories are full of numinous experiences, including the example of the Book of Kells, which begins this chapter. People who choose a career in museums often describe such experiences. But there are also cautionary tales illustrating how museums can provide transcendent moments and then snatch them away:

> I do have a horror story from my childhood, a museum horror story. . . At the Art Institute of Chicago. A museum I like a lot now but, of course I didn't have any experience with as a kid. . . . Anyway, this was probably fourth grade . . . I'd never been in such a place. And I was mesmerized. I was absolutely mesmerized. And I remember there was a docent, and the docent was pointing up and babbling away about a Mondrian that to me, at my height, was—I don't know, at least 20 feet up there. It made no sense. I didn't know what the woman was talking about. I'm sure it was important. And in front of me was a piece of sculpture. It's a piece of sculpture that tries to express this idea of horsepower. It is partly a horse's body, and it's partly mechanical, an engine. And so, there's a big flank of a horse with its leg sticking up with the hoof upside down on the thing. And then there's a deer. . . . And I instantaneously understood what this was about and was . . . just magnetized by it, and I reached out and touched it. The docent saw me. And the world came down around my ears. And I was a goody two-shoes. I mean, I couldn't stand any of this, you know. The teacher was incredibly embarrassed. . . . And I didn't ever step foot in that place again. And really, it was many years later before I would go to an art museum again" (M. Spock 2000b, 31).

Not surprisingly, children's museum professionals like Elaine Heumann Gurian were pioneers in acknowledging the significance of the emotional, reverential museum experience:

> Objects in exhibitions can elicit emotional responses. The presence of certain artifacts can evoke memories and feelings. . . . *If we are interested in changing our exhibitions into exhibitions of meaning, we will have to be prepared to include frankly emotional strategies* [emphasis added] (Gurian 1988, 181–82).

Gurian goes on to suggest that the reason museums have failed to acknowledge the sensory/affective nature of the experience lies within our Western intellectual traditions, which privilege language over the senses:

> [We share] certain cultural preferences for some modes of learning over others. For example, we have been taught that one mark of the civilized person is verbal ability, and so when explicating objects in, say, science or cultural-history museums, we concentrate on producing textual labels. Worst of all, appealing directly to the emotions is considered pandering to the mob, so we do not dare to appear enthusiastic (Gurian 1988, 183).

Gurian's thinking is not radical today, but when this article was published more than twenty years ago, it challenged the entrenched model of exhibition as transmitter of knowledge. Her point was to recognize the role of our senses in learning. (A more contemporary perspective, as I will discuss later, would be to bring all the senses, including the emotions, to the forefront of the entire experience.) This may reflect a more global shift in the cultural zeitgeist, including an enhanced respect for indigenous knowledge, the impact of neuroscience research, and the current focus on the bodily basis of cognition. But it is apparent that the senses, the emotions, and the imagination are officially on the agenda for museum talk. For instance, one of the major themes of the Museums Association's annual meeting (Great Britain) in 2013 was "the emotional museum":

> Is your museum devoid of emotion?
>
> Arguably the main reason that many museums worldwide are becoming more successful in attracting diverse audiences is that they have woken up to the fact that academic, sterile and dispassionate approaches to display are no longer acceptable to the public or funders.
>
> Museums need to become places where emotion is encouraged, where stories are told and where a visceral response is preferable to an intellectual one—more like places of worship (Museums Association 2013).

What portion of our visitors is looking for "a personal experience with something higher, more sacred, and out-of-the-ordinary than home and work are able to supply" (Graburn 1984, 180)? How would that compare to the desire for a social experience or an opportunity to learn something new? Do all three apply to everyone? And what about the people who don't visit museums at all? What can museums do to meet and satisfy these different motivations?

John Falk and Lynn Dierking have written that those seeking a reverential experience, whom they call Rechargers, represent a minority of visitors on any given day and are most likely to be found at art museums, botanical gardens, and aquariums (2012, 46). At the same time, they caution us not to "underestimate the emotional qualities of museums—feelings of awe and reverence are essential components of most people's museum experience. The emotions elicited, either intentionally or not, strongly influence resulting learning and meaning-making" (2012, 192).

Circling Back to the Education Model

The chapter has introduced some of the many ideas currently swirling around the field of exhibition development. A great many more—described with phrases like experience design, creativity, multiple modalities for learning, and twenty-first-century skills—appear in the literature and in panel presentations as the field continues to grapple with the nature of our most fundamental form of expression.[14] We have been nibbling away at the established assumption that exhibitions are about education, at least in the classic sense. But education remains nonetheless firmly established, and for some compelling reasons.

When *Teen Tokyo* opened at the Boston Children's Museum in 1992 (see chapter 1), my interview with the *Boston Globe* was published in the Learning section and titled "Exhibit as Education"—language we were thrilled to see. For decades, we had tried to convince the establishment, including the museum field, that our exhibitions were just that—playful experiences but with the serious intention of helping people learn about water, bubbles, or hydraulics; about the importance of play in early childhood; about estimating and scale; about cultures other than their own; and about themselves. It had been an uphill fight, and this article seemed to support that effort.[15]

But that was in the days before standardized testing and outcome-based evaluation became so entrenched. The education we offered was based firmly on John Dewey's principles of experiential learning, Lev Vygotsky's concept of scaffolding, the preeminence of play theory, and Howard Gardner's multiple-intelligence theory. It was process-based rather than outcome-based: learning about the nature and process of learning. The purpose of *Teen Tokyo* was to help

American youngsters see that they had a lot in common with their peers in this faraway place, while also beginning to probe the complexities of acculturation. I had little interest in teaching them facts about contemporary Japan.

Today it is much harder to avoid state and national curricular standards, including at children's museums. And at a so-called adult museum, where informal learning ideas may never have caught on in the past, the pressure can be even greater to establish quantifiable, measurable indices of what visitors learn. It requires creative and courageous thinking on the part of both funders and staff to define goals that genuinely reflect the true nature of the museum experience. This is not necessarily a bad thing. The more we are required to articulate why we do what we do, the better. Having to think about goals and objectives can be enlightening and even liberating. But it can also mean we are taking ourselves much too seriously (Rounds 2004). Like so many others, I do not think people come to museums determined to absorb what we have laboriously put out for them. Some do, of course, and many others are genuinely interested in learning either something new or confirming what they already understood.[16]

In any case, the field has more than enough scholars telling us how to ensure learning happens more often and with a more diverse range of visitors. Instead, I want to build on the notion that other things are happening in museum exhibitions than education or learning. Consider this adult's story of a childhood encounter with a diorama in a natural history museum:

> The really great [diorama] was the jaguar stalking the big rodent. And I couldn't read that word when I was a kid of what the animal was. And it was supposed to be someplace like Venezuela, but I thought that jungles were all in Brazil, so I thought it had to be Brazil. But it was neat to me. It was like seeing another way to paint, or another way to make a picture at least, to create this environment. And you could stand in front of it and just make up a whole story about what the bird that was sitting on the branch was going to do next, where that jaguar had come from, and, you know, did this big rodent have a family somewhere and was it out gathering food? I mean, there was this whole thing that you could fill in yourself about it, but that was really exciting (M. Spock 1992, 17.25; 2000c, 5).

I suggest that this encounter is about two important ideas, both tent poles for my own thinking, both closely allied: story and imagination. In the next three chapters I will explore these two concepts as well as the third, equally critical concept of aesthetic experience. Working together in what I call the subjunctive mood, these perspectives reveal the potential of exhibitions to be more than purely educational.

PART TWO

Constructing a New Model

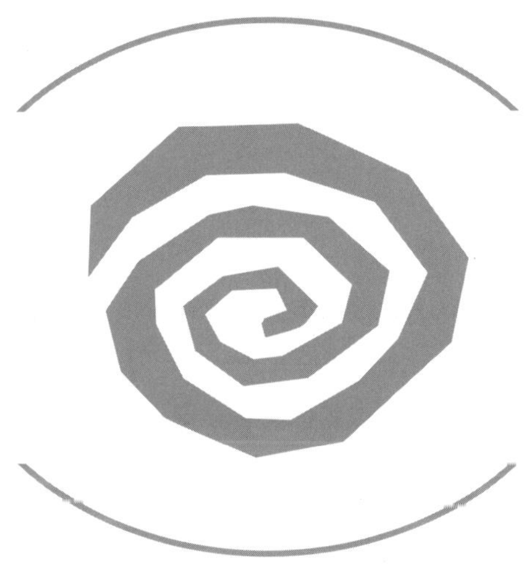

CHAPTER 3

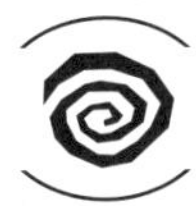

Story

> Some of my best memories are watching young people react to the history exhibits that we've done at the [United States] Holocaust [Memorial] Museum. Watching their responses to [it]—because we do have some places where kids or families, or adults, if they choose to, can interact and write things. . . . And I remember, it kind of made me come unglued at the same time, when I saw a note that was written by, I think, a ten-year-old girl named Charlotte. . . . We get many, many notes. But this one I remember in particular. . . . It was addressed to Daniel, the boy in *Daniel's Story*, through whose eyes you experience the history. . . . It said, "Dear Daniel, I feel so bad for you and your family and what happened to you. I wish I could bring them back. I think I've fallen in love with history." [1]

Most of us use the terms *story* and *narrative* interchangeably, but scholars distinguish between the two. They say that there are two parts to narrative: The story itself, fiction or nonfiction, is *what* happened at some time to someone in some place. The narrative, sometimes called narrative discourse, is *how* the story is told or represented by a particular medium, whether a book, film, video game or other interactive technology, newspaper article, painting, ballet, comic book, or exhibition. Story actually doesn't exist without an interpretative, a narrative discourse about it.

Leslie Bedford, "Story" in *The Art of Museum Exhibitions: How Story and Imagination Create Aesthetic Experiences*. pp. 57–64.

Narrative is a way of thinking about the world. In fact, it is the most fundamental way human beings think about themselves and their world, a phenomenon for which different disciplines have different explanations.

H. Porter Abbott (2002) points out that narrative begins as soon as youngsters, around age three or four, begin putting verbs together with nouns. They are telling a story. Since this is the same age as our earliest memories, he says, there is speculation that memory is itself dependent on this capacity for narrative (3). In any case, it is a fundamental, universal human characteristic and need; Abbott quotes novelist Paul Auster, who wrote that "a child's need for stories is as fundamental as his need for food" (Abbot 2002, 3).

What does story do for us? First of all, says Abbott, it gives us a way to organize time, a skill unique to our species. Because narrative provides a sense of causation, it also contributes a feeling of order in an essentially chaotic universe. Brian Boyd, a scholar of English literature, argues for a different evolutionary basis for this innate behavior. He says that creating stories—fiction—is a form of art and art a form of "cognitive play," which serves both individuals and society well. As a creative form, it both engages our love of finding pattern and generates new and productive ways of thinking; it helps us understand the who, what, and why of our and others' behavior. As such, it illustrates theory of mind, "a capacity to infer the beliefs, desires, and intentions of others and a self-awareness that allows us to understand how others might infer our motives and react to our moves" (Boyd 2009, 46). This capacity begins to appear during the second year of life and provides the foundations for future social interaction and growth. "Fictions foster cooperation by engaging and attuning our social and moral emotions and values," Boyd says, "and creativity by enticing us to think beyond the immediate in the way our minds are most naturally disposed—in terms of social actions" (2009, 383).

In any case, not only do we tell stories from a very early age, but we also search for them. The youngster focusing intently on the diorama of the South American rainforest (see chapter 2) illustrates the process well. He is looking for a narrative—a pattern— to make sense of the scene, and in so doing, he is creating his own story, one that relies on interpreting the behavior and motives of the animals he sees.

Lisa Roberts (see chapter 2) cites the contributions of cognitive psychologist Jerome Bruner, who also believes that narrative is an ineluctable part of being human. As mentioned earlier, Bruner distinguishes between two major modes of thought: the storytelling or narrative mode and the paradigmatic or logico-scientific mode. The latter draws on the Enlightenment faith in the supremacy of reason and the possibility of transmitting knowledge independent of context. This is the domain of science, math, and logic—of observable phenomena answerable to discernible and immutable laws. The narrative mode, Bruner argues, is the one people use to make sense of their world; it is subjective, interpretive, qualitative, and contextual. Both modes are natural to human thought, and both can be and are used to convince others. "Yet what they convince *of* is fundamentally different," he says. "Arguments convince one of their truth, stories of their lifelikeness" (Bruner 1986, 11; italics added).

The key point for Roberts is that the narrative mode is interpretive and interactive. Learning in the museum, she writes, has changed from signifying the transmission of knowledge from curator to the public to the sharing of narrative between educator and visitor. Narrative creates a conversation; it leads to an opening up—rather than a shutting down—of the listener's mind. Garrison Keillor, the master storyteller of National Public Radio's *Prairie Home Companion*, has written about the way the conversation works:

> I find that if I leave out enough details in my stories, the listener will fill in the blanks with her own hometown, and if a Freeport girl exiled in Manhattan hears the story about Memorial Day, she'll put it right there in that cemetery with those names on the stones, and she may think of her uncle Alcuin who went to France and didn't return and get out her hanky and blow. I'm not the reason she's moved, he is. All I do is say the words: cornfield and Mother and algebra and Chevy pickup and cold beer and Sunday morning and rhubarb and loneliness, and other people put pictures to them (Keillor 2000, 109).

In other words, storytelling, or the narrative mode of thought, is about *both* the storyteller *and* the listener (or viewer or visitor). Narrative stimulates personal interpretation; the person watching the film, reading the book, or experiencing the exhibition is engaged in his own kind of internal dialogue with the story. In this process of making meaning, he creates story out of story so that perceiving and creating become two sides of the same coin. The British scholar Chris Husbands puts it succinctly: "The telling of stories calls forth further stories" (1996, 51).

Finally, narratologists talk about something called narrativity, or the power to evoke story in the listener or viewer's mind. In other words, something does not have to be a formal story (with setting, action, and characters) in order to generate one. A piece of music can evoke a narrative. And so can objects, an insight to be explored later on. It is also true, of course, that some narratives—the ways in which a story is interpreted—have more narrativity than others, and this is due in part to the skill of the storyteller.

We do seem to be hard-wired for story. Or as the eighteenth-century Swiss physiologist Albrecht van Haller put it, "nature knits up her kinds in a network, not in a chain; but men follow only by chains because their language can't handle several things at once" (quoted in Steiner 2004, 145).

Story in the Museum

Finding and telling stories is so much a part of being human that it seems a natural, even critical strategy for museum programs and exhibitions. And story comes with an extra bonus: research shows that information received in story form is more easily absorbed and remembered.

Earlier chapters have referenced a few of the many narrative exhibitions in museums. For example, the Smithsonian's *From Field to Factory* offered a metanarrative, the story of the Great Migration of African Americans from the South to the North; *Choosing to Participate* subsumed four contemporary stories within a larger message of personal choices; the story of one boy, fictional but based on extensive research, is the framework for *Daniel's Story,* cited at the beginning of this chapter.

The exhibition *Open House: If These Walls Could Talk* also relies on storytelling. It was designed as a narrative over time with multiple stories, large and small, within the overarching master plot. According to Daniel Spock, who as head of exhibits at the Minnesota History Center oversaw the creation of *Open House*, the team consciously worked off the premise that "museum visitors most readily connect to history through the personal stories of others" (D. Spock 2007). What the summative evaluation shows is the essential interactive nature of story, how story generates story among visitors.

Something encountered in the exhibition—a photograph, kitchen table, or family movie—reminds visitors of a past they wish to share with their children, spouses, or friends. In the following dialogue, a 44-year-old woman

(M1) talks with her 14-year-old daughter (M2) in the first part of the exhibition, the 1880 parlor of a German immigrant family named Schumacher. They are looking at a three-dimensional "book" on coming to America which, when opened, reveals a kind of miniature diorama of objects relating to the Schumachers' sea voyage from Germany. This unusual exhibit prop inspires the mother to share the connection she makes to her own grandmother's immigrant experience:

> *M1:* If you look at this ship . . . come here . . .
>
> *M2:* Huh?
>
> *M1:* This is how all of our relatives came over . . . and I remember Grampa—You guys!—my Gramma was the one, she was the baby, 'cause her mom was pregnant when she came over on the ship. This here is talking about the people who built this house, the lady of the house was pregnant . . . and this is what they had to eat—'cause they weren't like the rich people on *Titanic*.
>
> *M2:* They just eat what they can?
>
> *M1:* Right. They were Germans, so they couldn't speak English.
>
> *M2:* They ate [bacon] and beans, or peas . . .
>
> [talking over each other about food]
>
> *M2:* Mmm, and the potatoes, too . . .
>
> *M1:* Well, potatoes are easy to bring on a ship.
>
> *M2:* Hm, cool. Wouldn't they be heavy, though, to carry?
>
> *M1:* Well, you just throw them all in the bottom of the ship . . . (Ellenbogen et al. 2006b, 89).

Because of its emotional resonance, story is often used in exhibitions for children, families, and more "visitor-centered" institutions. But it is also important to understand the deep connections between adults and storytelling. For example, Marsha Rossiter adopts the Bruner perspective—narrative as "a basic structure of human meaning making" (Rossiter 1999, 79)—and says that since narrative is by nature about memory and reflection, a narrative-based understanding of adult development makes sense. From a developmental perspective, adults are engaged in "rewriting the self" (Rossiter 1999, 81).

This perspective can be inferred to some extent from the Philadelphia Stories, which are often personal rewritings of the self. The respondents were asked, for instance, to relate a memorable learning experience in a museum, and they often obliged at considerable length. While there are a number of stories of adult experiences, the majority are recollections from childhood, such as:

> Art museums were anchors and beacons, and the paintings in them were friends I had conversations with and I always go back to. . . . I still remember the paintings I saw when I was that age, and how much they came to life. They were objects that I had conversations with, you know, that I could go back to all the time and have conversations with.
>
> And I remember them being flat. It wasn't as though they were windows onto another world. It wasn't as though it were something I could step into. But my whole sense of scale and feelings and perception, my whole sense of perception was shaped by the real physicality of these objects.
>
> And of course, there was a very rich fantasy life around them, and I think there was something about the kind of dialogue or one-on-one conversation I could construct with them, and around them, that really meant a great deal to me, and somehow resolved the completely unresolvable conflict about the different messages I was getting at an early age from my family. . . . I think they were anchors because it was a place that felt stable and a place where my questions that weren't getting answered, could somehow be played out" (M. Spock 1992, 58–02).

An axiom in adult learning theory holds that adults are even more individualistic than children because they have been shaped by many more years of experience. Each successive act of imaginative restorying of experience lays down another layer of meaning.

The adult development perspective raises interesting possibilities for museums. Adults may bring not only their capacity for imagination but also their ongoing personal narratives to the exhibition experience, which may in turn inspire the creation of more story. An example of this kind of process comes from the Philadelphia Stories:

> And at times in my life where I've . . . needed some kind of calming, like right after my divorce, I took a course at the [American] Museum of Natural History . . . where all you did was sit in front of those

> exhibits, the exact same exhibits from my childhood, and draw. And it was kind of like a meditation. It was like you'd get deep inside yourself as you sat sort of voiceless, in front of these dioramas . . . that went back so deeply into my life, which I already had several experiences with as a child and as an adolescent, and just sketch them, so you'd be able to begin to see them in a new way: from the childhood to the adult way of seeing (M. Spock 1992, 14.10; 2000c).

This story, of course, also recalls the therapeutic role of museums that Lois Silverman highlights in *The Social Work Of Museums* (2010).

In the following example, an adult is engaged in using her imagination—clearly a fertile one—to create a narrative that weaves the experience of visiting Paul Revere's house into her own history and understanding of self. From a diary entry regarding a museum visit by a 21-year-old student who wants to become an opera singer, it is worth quoting in its entirety:

> . . . When we first saw his house I was filled with awe because Paul Revere actually lived here. This was the house he returned to after staying up all night chopping open chests and dumping tea into Boston Harbor. This was the house he left to make his famous night ride, and this was the house the many spies reported things to him in the months leading up to the war came to . . .
>
> When I saw the house's front entry, which was barely big enough for one person to stand in, and the stairs which were incredibly small and cramped and delicate, I realized the house was much too small to have held all of Paul's children . . . and his wife and mother comfortably. It occurred to me that he could not have had any privacy back then. . . . I suppose people back then weren't shocked by much. Paul was such an easygoing person I'm sure it never occurred to him to worry about what people saw him doing. . . .
>
> Paul was by all accounts an extremely competent and practically minded person, so he would have fit in well. However, I doubt I would have fit in to his time very well. I don't think I would have had a very high opinion of myself if I lived then, because I would have had little opportunity for mastery, and I might never have known that I have certain skills . . . I also have extremely little patience for repetitive tasks, but "women's work" was filled with them. . . . If I had been Paul

> Revere's daughter I would have learned to read and write a little, and I am good at those things so I would have taken pride in that . . . I would still be able to sing well, although I would never be able to sing as well as I do now because I wouldn't have had singing lessons. . . . Of course I never would have been sent to college back then. Girls had absolutely no choice about what they would do when they grew up. . . . All men back then were sexist, but I don't get the impression Paul was especially so. . . .
>
> After touring the house and discovering how dreadfully practical life was in Paul Revere's day, I was shocked to see some of his silver work. . . . His work took my breath away because of the sharp contrast between it and the no-frills environment he lived in. It was delicate and intricate down to the last detail. . . . Paul wanted his work to be as beautiful as he could make it. . . . So this practical man got his greatest joy out of making something impractical. He was a lot more like me than I thought (quoted in Leinhardt et al. 2000, 115, 120–21).

A preference for story argues against the conventional wisdom that visitors need choices and dislike having to follow a single chronological line. This is an important point. However, not every story is a narrative. Too often history museums fall back on the storylike, what I once called "didactic wolves dressed in storyteller sheep's clothing"—exhibitions with titles such as "The Story of Colonial New England" (Bedford 2001, 33). These exhibitions may be stories; there are characters, a setting, and action. But they are not true narratives; they do not take the listener/visitor to another place in his mind; they do not engage her emotions or imagination. A narrative has to be true to its medium. For exhibition makers, that means engaging all our senses including the somatic or physical, speaking to our emotions, using the specific to generate connections to the familiar and universal, and telling us something about someone we are going to care about. Something happens in the imagination in the face of a real story; it creates a new one.

CHAPTER 4

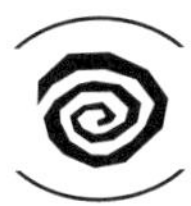

Imagination

> I remember going to this really horrible little museum . . . when I was a kid. . . . It was like a junk store almost, things on racks. And you could touch everything, which is kind of weird. They had a rack of old guns, and one of them, they said, was Daniel Boone's. And I thought that was pretty wild. And you could touch it. And I couldn't believe how huge it was. And I could put my thumb into the opening of the barrel. And I thought, man, that's a big, heavy thing to be hauling around all day. I thought that this must have been hard work, being like one of these mountain guys. It wasn't like Kirk Douglas, you know, beating his chest and grinning, wandering around in the woods and carefree. It looked like a chore to haul this big gun and a big knife and, you know, load the thing. And just being able to handle it meant a lot (M. Spock 1992, 17.26; 1999b, 9; 2000b, 1).

Like many people, I once thought about story as separate from the imagination. I knew stories were generative, that they stoked the active mind that educational theorists urged us to address, but I failed to recognize the imagination's starring role in their creation. Fortunately, the two began to come together in the mid-1990s when I was shaping a rationale for our programs at the Brooklyn Historical Society. Maureen Ott, a colleague from the Minnesota History Center, sent me an article called "Accumulating History," by the Welsh-born Canadian scholar Kieran Egan. I had majored in history in college but never encountered his developmental approach to the teaching and

Leslie Bedford, "Imagination" in *The Art of Museum Exhibitions: How Story and Imagination Create Aesthetic Experiences*. pp. 65–76.

learning of history. It struck me as ideal for a history museum serving all ages. My team and I used Egan's framework to create the small and inexpensive exhibition about Jackie Robinson and the Brooklyn Dodgers mentioned in the introduction, an obvious choice for the setting. *Playball!* garnered publicity in the *New York Times* and laid the groundwork for a new institutional direction in exhibitions.

Egan's article turned out to be the tip of the iceberg for an entire philosophy called *imaginative education*. The mission of the Imaginative Education Research Group (IERG),[1] which Egan founded in 2001, is to reform classroom teaching; the title of one article, "Start Not with What the Student Knows but What He Can Imagine," sums it up well.

Many disciplinary lenses are available to analyze the imagination—aesthetics, psychology, philosophy, literature—but imaginative education's approach, despite its focus on schools, is particularly relevant to museum work because it gives practitioners clear concepts and concrete strategies for engaging the learner's imagination and thus his creativity.[2] Although imaginative education has shown up more and more in writings and panels on museum education, it merits a closer look than some of the other, more familiar approaches I discussed in earlier chapters.

A good place to start is with Egan's definition of imagination itself. In his *A Very Short History of Imagination* (2007), he reviews how Western civilization—theologians, philosophers, psychologists, artists, educators, and cognitive scientists—has tried to understand the workings of the imagination. These various perspectives continue to influence our thinking about the imagination in ways we may not be aware of. Starting with the Judeo-Christian and classical traditions, imagination was not admired. Creativity—thinking in alternative ways—was considered a rebellion against divine order and later as a merely ornamental and inauthentic faculty that involved "the lower parts of our nature" (Egan 2007, 4). The thinkers of the Scientific Revolution in the seventeenth century considered imagination as suitable only for poetry, art, or children and of no use in the higher realm of scientific reasoning. It took first the Enlightenment and then the romantic poets to revise this dismissive, even hostile perspective. In the early to mid-nineteenth century, Samuel Coleridge, William Wordsworth, William Blake, and others cited the imagination's generative powers to "[shape] the world we perceive and . . . [use] our hopes, fears, and other emotions in that shaping" (Egan 2007, 10).

In the last century, philosophers and practitioners of the new field of psychology weighed in. Philosophers like Jean-Paul Sartre argued that the imagination is "an intentional act of consciousness rather than a thing in consciousness" (Egan 2007, 12)—in other words, a process and not a faculty. His English contemporary I. A. Richards agreed, reframing the imagination as "the active mind, the mind in action construing and constructing, dissolving and re-creating, making sense, making meaning" (Egan 2007, 13). Significantly though not surprisingly, in connecting the work of the imagination with the concept of an active mind, we have thus arrived nearer to the constructivist, meaning-making model that Lisa Roberts, George Hein, Lois Silverman, and others employ in analyzing museum learning.

After a detailed discussion of the fallacy of conflating imagination with visualization—it is much more than simply the creation of images—and a respectful nod to his many predecessors, Egan and his Imaginative Education Research Group crafted the following definition:

> [Imagination] is the ability to think of the possible, not just the actual; it is the source of invention, novelty, and flexibility in human thinking; it is not distinct from rationality but is rather a capacity that greatly enriches rational thinking; it is tied to our ability to form images in the mind, and image-forming commonly involves emotions (IERG 2013).

What I find critical and most valuable about this definition is how it integrates reason, visual images, and emotions, and credits imagination as the source of "invention, novelty, and flexibility in human thinking." It is a highly generative, active faculty—for Egan, the very heart of learning, central to every kind of content, not simply the arts with which it is more conventionally linked. Or to paraphrase another scholar, imagination might be seen as "thought's direction" (Sutton-Smith 1988, 7).

How Imaginative Education Works

Egan explains the two theoretical foundations for imaginative education in *The Educated Mind* (1997). The first is a reframing of the theory of cultural recapitulation, which says that students can learn the thinking tools invented during eons of human history over their own lifetimes. The second draws on the sociocultural theories of the Russian psychologist Lev Vygotsky:

> It is not that something that occurred in cultural history causes an aptitude in every child to acquire knowledge in the same order, but rather than acquiring specific intellectual tools, the modern individual generates similar kinds of understanding as existed for people using those tools in the past (Egan 1997, 30).

He links these kinds of understanding to a process of culturally accumulated complexity in language, beginning with oral language (Mythic), then moving to literacy (Romantic), then to the development of systematic, abstract, theoretic, linguistic forms (Philosophic), and finally to habitual, highly reflexive uses of language (Ironic). But before these understandings can develop, there is an earlier and more fundamental understanding, the Somatic, which comes from embodied knowledge (the senses) and continues to develop within the other understandings throughout the lifespan.

The separate understandings generally develop in sequence, appearing as new linguistic skills are mastered and coalescing, as each successive kind has emerged. While usually corresponding to specific ages, the understandings do not just appear naturally at a particular age in some steady and inevitable process; this is not human development theory. Nor do they disappear as new understandings and tools appear. The modern mind is thus a kind of composite of the five understandings. We are a "five-minded animal, in whom the different kinds of understanding jostle together and fold in on one another, to some degree coalescing, to some degree remaining 'somewhat distinct' " (Egan 1997, 180).

Each understanding is accompanied by a different set of concrete "cognitive tools," which we use to think. To explain this term, Egan likes to tell a story about early man. He conjures up an image of an old guy sitting under a tree somewhere in the plains of Africa. A crowd gathers around in admiration and gratitude: he has just invented the past tense. And then two weeks later, his clever daughters come up with the subjunctive mood and metaphor. He asks us to imagine living without the past tense or the ability to ask "what if?"

A look at the different understandings illustrated by some of the Philadelphia Stories clarifies why and how they can work within the museum context.

Somatic understanding is about understanding experience in a physical, prelinguistic way. Information comes through the senses as our physical bodies interact with the environment. It employs the tools of the senses, or the "body's toolkit" as well as emotional response, mimesis, and intentionality.

Egan writes about how all our later ability to make meaning derives from—and often continues to depend on—our initial, infantile explorations with our bodies. Somatic understanding has much in common with another concept, "embodied imagination," which is discussed in greater detail below. A typical example of the Somatic in a museum setting is the story about Daniel Boone's gun that opens this chapter. By simply lifting and holding this enormous object, the youngster is able, through his body, to imagine himself as another, adult person in another age.

Mythic understanding refers to understanding experience through oral language, which appeared with evolutionary changes in human physiognomy. As Egan points out, words must have seemed powerful and magical at first. This acquisition of language allowed us to discuss, represent, and understand things even if they are not actually experienced in person. The tools available include story structuring, metaphor, joking and humor, abstract binary opposites, forming images from words, rhyme, rhythm and pattern, games, drama and play, and a sense of mystery (Egan 1997, 33–70).

According to Egan and imaginative education, children respond to binary opposites from an early age and use them to create and learn through stories. Big and small, good and evil, old and young are the stuff of fairy tales and myths. Much of the power of *Daniel's Story* at the United States Holocaust Memorial Museum (the example at the beginning of chapter 3) comes from its Mythic storytelling, the stark and deeply emotional contrast between Daniel's early life in a comfortable, loving home and the horrors of existence in the ghetto.

Daniel's Story also illustrates the use of cognitive tools from Romantic understanding, which is about grasping experience through the tools associated with literacy. The child experiences growing independence and separateness from a world that appears increasingly complex. He relates readily to extremes of reality, associates with heroes, and seeks to make sense of the world in human terms. The tools thus include the sense of reality, a focus on the extremes of experience and the limits of reality, an association with heroes, a sense of wonder, seeing knowledge in human terms, collections and hobbies, revolt and idealism, role-play, and narrative understanding (Egan 1997, 81–97). The Jackie Robinson exhibition at the Brooklyn Historical Society in the mid-1990s spoke quite intentionally to the Romantic: Robinson was both real and heroic.

Philosophic understanding refers to the management of experience through the theoretic use of language. Its tools include the sense of abstract reality, the sense of agency, a grasp of general ideas and their anomalies, the search for authority and truth, and metanarrative understanding. The Philosophic mind is involved with finding connections and "constructing theories, laws, ideologies, and metaphysical schemes" (Egan 1997, 121). This kind of understanding is expressly nurtured in secondary school. It is also most likely to show up in exhibitions for adult audiences on the assumption—mistaken, in my opinion—that we all work comfortably with abstraction, agency, and metanarratives. Illustrating as they do the narrative rather than the paradigmatic mode of thinking, the Philadelphia Stories revealed few if any Philosophic tools at work. But the *Open House* exhibition conversations provide numerous examples of pairs of adult visitors using their "capacity to think of things as possibly being so" to make comparisons between past and present, and thus construct a kind of metanarrative of change over time.[3]

In the following, a 59-year-old woman (M1) and a (barely audible) 34-year-old man (M2) converse as they visit the last room in an exhibition which is designed to highlight the lifestyle of several generations of Hmong immigrants, who are the current occupants of the actual house. In this conversation, they use the evidence from their visit to think on an abstract level and begin to construct theories of neighborhood change using the evidence they have found in the exhibition—or that they have brought to the experience—to do so:

> *M1:* Had you seen . . . how the East Side changed over the years?
>
> (video audio)
>
> *M1:* It must have always been kind of cheaper housing, or something? Cheaper housing on the East Side or something?
>
> *M2:* (inaudible) . . .
>
> *M1:* Do they have pets? . . . I don't know . . . (name) used to live on the East Side, and she was . . . they weren't poor. . . .
>
> *M2:* No, even back before they built the house it was a poor neighborhood . . . (Ellenbogen et al. 2006, 64).

Finally, Egan describes an Ironic understanding achieved through the reflexive use of language. This kind of understanding acknowledges the limits to systematic thinking, including language, in capturing what is important about the world, and it believes that the way we make sense of the world depends on our unique historical and cultural perspective. Its tools include the limits of theory, reflexivity and identity, coalescence, particularity, and radical epistemic doubt (Egan 1997, 155–62). Egan isn't a relativist or a cynic; he is talking about the mind of an adult who has moved beyond excessive rationality and recognized the "contingency of things" and the inherent wisdom of multiple perspectives.

One can discern the Ironic—and the Somatic as well—in the following example from the Philadelphia Stories about a visit to the Babe Ruth Museum. Without knowing exactly how old the speaker was at the time, one wonders if this is a young adult who is already comfortable with multiple interpretations or a mature man using the tools of Ironic understanding to recall and make meaning of a youthful experience:

> The scene is the Babe Ruth Museum, which is a small historic house in Baltimore, near where Camden Yards, the baseball park, is now. And I'm not a great baseball fan, but I like night baseball. So I went with my family, my father and my mother. I flashed my Smithsonian I.D. so I didn't have to pay at the door. I walked in and you come to a gift counter. Behind the gift counter was the director, curator, gift shop manager, and custodian, all of them the same person. And went into the living room, and he saw my Smithsonian I.D., and so there was some sort of collegial connection, and he said, "Wait here a minute." And he went into the closet and came out with two bats. And he handed me one and he said, "This is Jackie Robinson's bat."
>
> And so, I'm standing now in Babe Ruth's living room, swinging Jackie Robinson's bat, trying not to hit the lamps in the living room, right? And then, so he takes that one away. And he hands me the next one. He goes, "This is Babe Ruth's bat." Now, Babe Ruth's bat was a fifty-four ounce bat, which is a very heavy baseball bat. Most baseball bats are thirty to forty ounces. So, it's like a piece of iron. It weighs a ton. And so here, in what looked to be the same room that Babe Ruth grew up in, I'm holding and taking licks with Babe Ruth's bat.
>
> And now, particularly in light of all this DNA discussion—I mean, somewhere on that bat is sort of his DNA and my DNA, at the same place, at the same time. What was affecting about that, that not only did they trust me not to hit anything with the bat, but there was a direct connection to what that bat was all about, why that bat was important (M. Spock 1992, 17.6–7; 2000b, 19).

Imaginative Education and Museums

Imaginative education has much to offer the museum field. First, it gives us a framework for making decisions about interpretive strategies. So just as exhibition developers in children's and science museums often turn to child development theory, Vygotsky's notion of a zone of proximal development, or Csikszentmihalyi's theory of flow, they can add Egan's taxonomy to their planning toolkits as we did at the Brooklyn Historical Society with the Jackie Robinson exhibition.

Second, imaginative education is appropriate to museums' intergenerational audiences. As Egan says, we are "five-minded." As a person matures through language from Mythic to Romantic or Romantic to Philosophic and Ironic, the adult doesn't lose his earlier tools; he simply uses them in new ways. Some of these conceptual tools can thus function not unlike the principles of universal design, where, for instance, touchable objects enlighten the sighted visitor as well as the visually impaired, for whom they are more typically displayed.

This insight applies especially vividly to two sets of imaginative education's cognitive tools: those associated with story and those we get from our bodies. Before they can read, youngsters will respond to story through the tool of binary opposites. As they move into Romantic understanding, they continue to embrace story but now are looking for real-life heroes and extremes. As secondary school students, they continue to use story, including historical and other metanarratives. For Egan and his colleagues, the first question teachers should ask of any new content is, "What's the story?" How can one turn this information into a story with emotional impact? In encountering imaginative education, I found reinforcement for my early embrace of narrative in exhibitions. I had come to it initially through other routes, both theoretical and practical, but now I had a convincing rationale and methodology for applying it.

The second set of tools, the so-called "body's toolkit," merits further treatment because it relates to the extraordinary recent advances in cognitive science and neuroscience, which argue for an "embodied" or "situated" approach to human cognition, behavior, and imagination.

When the Boston Children's Museum design team created *Teen Tokyo* in 1991, we wanted to include a range of hands-on experiences; that was, after all, the calling card and holy grail of the children's museum field. We knew hands-on "worked" from years of experience, but we also had heard of Howard Gardner's multiple intelligence theory, including kinesthetic intelligence.

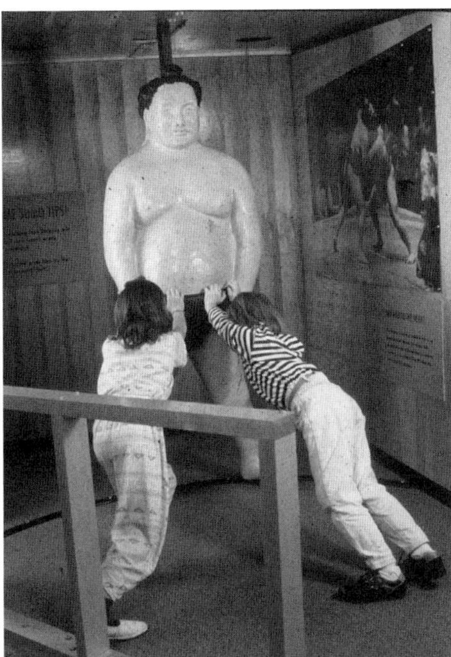

Teen Tokyo included a giant sumo wrestler; children loved to push him out of his ring. Photo courtesy of Boston Children's Museum.

Several of us had visited *Inside Ancient Egypt* at the Field Museum, where our former colleague Janet Kamien had installed a huge stone attached to ropes, inviting visitors to drag the stone and see what it was like to build the pyramids. So we worked hard to create physical experiences. For instance, we designed a huge, weighted sumo wrestler for visitors to try to push out of his ring. The constant need to clean his glossy surface testified to his popularity.

The following story is one I related about another element of this exhibition: an authentic Japanese subway car. It also speaks to experience based in the physical, the Somatic, but in this case, by creating the illusion of sensations:

> *Teen Tokyo* . . . has a very fancy, expensive subway car which cost $50,000. And we had a big debate as to whether it was worth having it. . . . And I argued for the subway car. And we did evaluations to see what we would have to do to make people believe in the subway car. Because we couldn't have the doors open and shut. We couldn't have it really move.
>
> So, we did things. We had sound under the seats, and we had lights going by, and we had the sound overhead of a Japanese conductor. And I saw this kid come out of the subway car and just stagger,

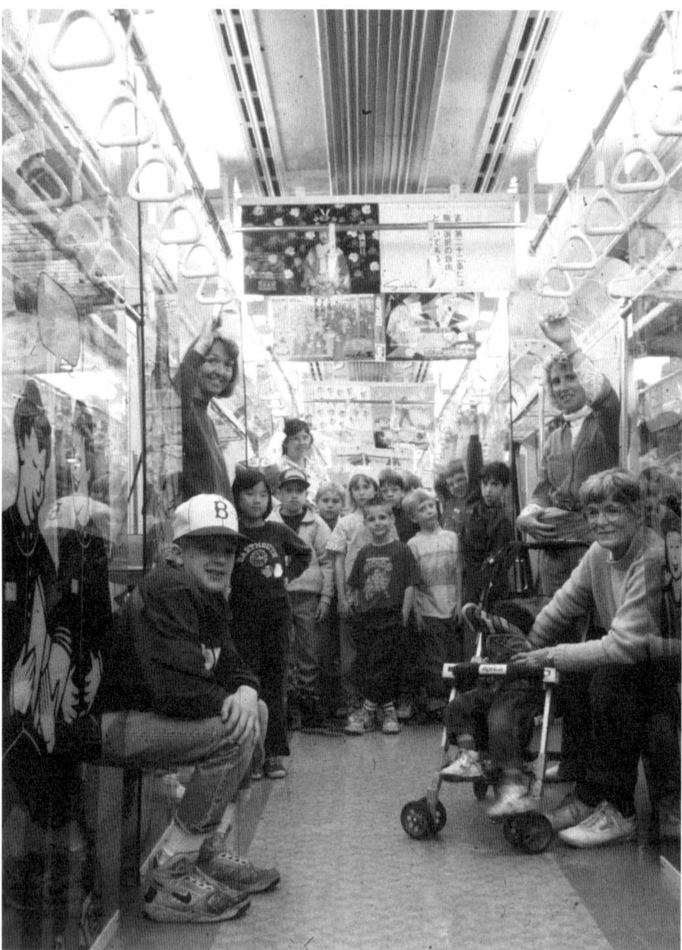

The highly realistic subway car in *Teen Tokyo* was fabricated by a subway company in Kobe, Japan, and was outfitted with sounds, feet drawn on the floor to give the feeling of crowded space, and a cast of fanciful fellow riders. Photo courtesy of Boston Children's Museum.

you know, like he was getting off a moving subway car. And he was having such a good time. And I thought, "Bingo. We've provided this. . . ." I don't know really what was going on. But it felt like this kid had been transported someplace else in his imagination and that we had allowed that to happen, which is something I think museums can do (M. Spock 1992, 13.3–4; Spock and Leichter 1999, 45–46).

Since then, our understanding of hands-on or Somatic understanding and tools has benefited from many years of substantial research about the fundamental connection between mind and body. This research has inevitably found its way into the museum world. As Jonathan Hale, an architect, scholar, and co-editor of *Museum Making: Narratives, Architectures, Exhibitions*, writes, "a new appreciation has emerged, across a broad range of fields, of the fact that human beings are essentially embodied creatures" (Hale 2012, 92). At the American Alliance of Museums' 2013 annual meeting, Reach Advisors collaborated with the Johns Hopkins Medicine Brain Science Institute in examining the relevance of embodied imagination to museum practice. There will be much more in the future. In the meantime, what are some of the big ideas for our practice?

The main point, of course, is that the mind and body work together. Sandra Blakeslee and Matthew Blakeslee, authors of *The Body Has a Mind of its Own* [4] put it this way:

> Your body is not just a vehicle for your brain to cruise around in. The relationship is perfectly reciprocal: Your body and your brain exist for each other. A body that can be moved or stilled, touched or evaded, scalded or warmed, frozen or cooled, strained or rested, starved, devoured, or nourished, is the raison d'être of the senses. And the sensations from your skin and body—touch, temperature, pain, and a few others you will learn about—are your mind's true foundation (Blakeslee and Blakeslee 2008, 12).

Two body maps help us determine how we feel in and about our bodies. One is the body schema, or "felt sense," an unconscious, physiological construct created by the brain from the interaction of our senses. It includes our "peripersonal" space, the bubble that surrounds our body and can be extended through tools like a broom or a cane for the blind. Dancers, athletes, and healers exemplify people with finely tuned senses of peripersonal space. The other body map, called body image, is our more conscious perception of our body and how we present it to others. The interaction of the body schema and the body image is an ongoing and constructivist process. The brain is constantly comparing incoming information to what it already knows or expects or believes. "As higher areas make sense of the input—'Yes, this is something I have seen before'—the information is fed back to lower areas to confirm that what you believe is happening really is happening" (Blakeslee and Blakeslee 2008, 41).

In other words, our perceptions are conditioned by past experience. And because experience and therefore our expectations and beliefs shape what we see, hear, feel, and think, our "understanding of reality is a far cry from reality itself" (Blakeslee and Blakeslee 2008, 41–42). Inevitably, culture deeply shapes perception.

Perception is also multisensory. Our senses interact with each other so that, for example, we will see something faster if it also makes a sound, and hear better if we can see who is speaking. And this is true if the sense is outside your body but within your peripersonal space. As we all know, you can make a child giggle by simply wriggling your fingers near his stomach (Blakeslee and Blakeslee 2008, 116–117).

Finally, the way we process information isn't just shaped by doing something physically with our bodies. Thinking about, imagining, and seeing someone else do a familiar action also affects us physically, and thus mentally. This is the work of mirror neurons, "the body maps that run simulations of what other people's body maps are up to" (Blakeslee and Blakeslee 2008, 166). By modeling or simulating what other people are doing, feeling, intending, they help us get inside their minds. "They allow you to grasp the minds of others, not through conceptual reasoning but by modeling their actions, intentions, and emotions in the matrix of your own body mandala" (Blakeslee and Blakeslee 2008, 166).

Mirror neurons enable us to understand and empathize with others. Someone breaks down in tears or begins smiling broadly, and we register sadness or happiness in our own bodies and minds. A baby starts to cry when he hears another crying, and "a knock on the door has the same effect on your brain whether you hear it, see it or do it yourself" (Blakeslee and Blakeslee 2008, 170–72).

We have come a long way since the days when mind and body—like imagination and reason—were considered distinct and unequal aspects of humanity. Now we know they cannot be separated. Story, imagination, and the body are parts of a whole. Each reinforces the power of the others and each ultimately brings one back to the emotions. And all three belong to the making and experiencing of exhibitions. Exhibitions can reinforce the experience, the narrative, through the interaction of multiple bodily senses. Those at a "high level of narrativity," such as immersive exhibitions, can become opportunities for the visitor to be so "sufficiently engaged [that] they can become an actor in the story-world and move themselves through the story, shifting from conscious to unconscious engagement depending on their own narrativization of self" (Blakeslee and Blakeslee 2008, 109).

Chapter 5

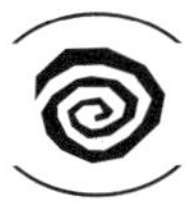

John Dewey and Art as Experience

> I remember very distinctly walking into one of the reconstructed Egyptian tombs at the Metropolitan Museum for the hundredth time, and realizing on a visceral level for the first time that a human being had made those walls. And I was standing next to walls that someone had made thousands of years ago. And it was electrifying. It was a moment that could not have happened in virtuality. It had to happen in the physical world. It was very unexpected, because there was nothing new about the experience, but it was very powerful (M. Spock 1992, 18.7).

Philosopher John Dewey (1859–1952) had incalculable influence on educational theory and practice in the twentieth century, including in museums. He incorporated frequent museum visits into the curriculum for the lab school he and his wife founded at the University of Chicago, and he later worked closely with businessman, collector, and founder of the Barnes Foundation Dr. Albert C. Barnes, to whom he dedicated *Art as Experience* in 1934. His philosophy of education placed experience at the center of teaching and learning, which he reframed as "learning through doing." This philosophy shaped the revolutionary work of the Boston Children's Museum and San Francisco's Exploratorium beginning in the 1960s, as well as a half-century of experiential exhibitions in museums. A more recent trend, the museum field's focus on community or civic engagement, also evokes Dewey and the progressive movement's commitment to participatory democracy. And Dewey's insistence that education encompasses what comes before a learning experience as well as after—the concept of continuity of experience—reverberates with such current constructivist theory as John Falk and Lynn Dierking's contextual model of learning (see chapter 2).[1]

For me, coming first from the Dewey-inspired Boston Children's Museum (learning through doing) and then teaching at the Dewey-reverential Bank Street College of Education (learner-centered education), these ideas resonate deeply and seem irrefutable. This chapter explores Dewey's philosophy as well as Maxine Greene's belief in the transformative power of personal engagement with works of art, and Mihaly Csikszentmihalyi's insistence that aesthetic experiences yield happiness and cannot be subjected to conventional cognitive assessment. They all open up opportunities for a new way of thinking about the medium of exhibitions, one that is much more appropriate to our current belief in meaning making than it was to an older, if still prevalent, commitment to the transmission of knowledge and education.

The Aesthetic Experience Unpacked

Dewey's masterwork, *Art as Experience* (1934), relates most convincingly to exhibition development. His writings are dense and convoluted, and *Art as Experience* is not an easy read. Other scholars—including Philip W. Jackson (1998) and George Hein (2004, 2006a, 2012)—help us identify the salient and most relevant among Dewey's many important ideas.

For Dewey, an aesthetic experience is—or more accurately, *should be*—part of everyday life. In fact, as he noted in a 1938 talk to the Washington Dance Association, if aesthetic experiences were more common, we could stop labeling them "aesthetic": "We should know it for what it is—simply experience itself, having experiences at their best and at their fullest" (Dewey 1938, 368). Art, he maintains, has always been continuous with everyday life; philosophers and art museums are responsible for putting it on a conceptual pedestal out of the ordinary person's reach.[2]

Dewey devoted his life to seeking "a unifying theme that might be applicable to all traditional philosophical questions—logic, ethics, metaphysics, aesthetics, and so on" (Hein 2006a, 183). He was a "both-and" thinker: Ideas exist along a continuum of theory and practice, in this case, one of making and appreciating art. Dualities—"either-or"—invite comparison and thus hierarchy. So for Dewey, classic Western dualities—art and science, theory and practice, mind and body—are false and harmful.

Because it is continuous with life, we can know the experience of art just as we can any other kind of experience. The driving force behind Dewey's philosophy was his commitment to social democracy, so he had little patience for elitist aestheticism: "Esthetics does not dictate how materials are to be used, other than to say, 'Esthetically!'—that is, for the enrichment of immediate experience" (Kaplan 1981, xxiii). But art offers more than simple experience. It offers "*an* experience," one that is "educative," that leads to growth and does "something to prepare a person for later experience of a deeper and more expansive quality" (quoted in Jackson 1998, 6). *An* experience draws on what came before and leads to what comes after, or, as Dewey puts it, "Art celebrates with peculiar intensity the moments in which the past reenforces the present and in which the future is a quickening of what now is" (Dewey 1934, 18). Human beings have experiences all the time—brushing one's teeth is an experience—but it is not educative, not *an* experience in a Deweyian sense.[3]

This continuity exists *within* the experience as well:

> Because of continuous merging, there are no holes, mechanical junctions, and dead centers when we have *an* experience. There are pauses, places of rest, but they punctuate and define the quality of movement. They sum up what has been undergone and prevent its dissipation and idle evaporation (Dewey 1934 [1959], 36).

Such an experience is about both the artist's "product" and also the person encountering it; it is the interaction that creates the work of art:

> The *product* of art—temple, painting, statue, poem—is not the *work* of art. The work takes place when a human being cooperates with the product so that the outcome is an experience that is enjoyed because of its liberating and ordered properties (Dewey 1934 [1959], 214).

As the result of *an* experience, both the person who experiences *and* the object experienced are irrevocably changed:

> The experiencer changes by undergoing a transformation of the self, gaining a broadened perspective, a shift of attitude, an increase of knowledge, or any of a host of other enduring alterations of psychological nature. The object of experience changes through the acquisition of new meanings (Jackson 1998, 5–6).

Aesthetic experiences exist along a continuum. Some can be truly transcendent and life changing—the encounter with Botticelli's paintings from chapter 2—and others may partake of the aesthetic but are not purposefully so—like the experience of a beautiful sunset. But according to Dewey, all experiences share three characteristics:

1. *Completeness.* An experience neither fades out nor comes to a sudden end. It has closure. It can be something as ordinary as a good meal or as transformative as a visit to Chartres Cathedral, but always the experience comes to a close:

   > We have *an* experience when the material experienced runs its courses to fulfillment. Then and then only is it integrated within and demarcated in the general stream of experience from other experiences. . . . Such an experience is a whole and carries with it its own individualizing quality and self-sufficiency (Dewey 1934 [1959], 35).

2. *Uniqueness.* Each such experience is unique and whole. It cannot be taken apart and analyzed, at least not while it is occurring. Jackson vividly illustrates this point through a story by Annie Dillard. She describes her experience of stopping at a rural gas station, where she finds herself stroking the fur of the owner's puppy, watching the sunset over the mountains, and smelling the loam. And then she writes: "And the second I verbalize this awareness in my brain, I cease to see the mountain or feel the puppy. I am opaque, so much black asphalt" (quoted in Jackson 1998, 17–18). Self-awareness has brought the experience to an end. Dillard is talking about something students of museum education will recognize as "flow," the state of mind so brilliantly captured by psychologist Mihaly Csikszentmihalyi. The experience that comes after this moment, however, is also valuable—if not aesthetic—in Deweyian terms because it constitutes the reflection that continues the experience and reinforces its educational value.
3. *Unifying emotion.* We do not experience emotions independent of the context that gave them their meaning. According to Dewey, "experience is emotional but there are no separate things called emotions in it" (1934, 42). Rather, emotion holds an experience together, and its unity provides the aesthetic experience.

But while Dewey insisted that aesthetic experience was congruent with everyday life, *Art as Experience* looks at works of art rather than sunsets. In seeking to clarify what the points along Dewey's continuum might be, Jackson draws a clear distinction between "art-centered experiences"—those focused on works of art—and others of a more generic or natural nature. The former, he says, are qualitatively different[4] and involve understanding two key concepts: perception vs. recognition, and expansion of meaning.

Dewey makes a critical distinction between perception and recognition. In *recognizing* an object, for example, one is thinking about how it might be used for some purpose outside the immediate experience. Perception is different: "To perceive an object is not simply to see, hear, smell, taste, or touch it. It is to make sense of what one senses, to partake of its meaning" (Jackson 1998, 57). It involves our entire self. Thus "recognition is perception arrested before it has a chance to develop freely. . . . In recognition we fall back, as upon a stereotype, upon some previously formed scheme" (Dewey 1934 [1959], 52). But in the arts, the object is worthy of attention on its own; it has intrinsic value.

Expansion of meaning refers to the open-ended nature of perception. "There is always more to see, or hear, or touch, or smell, or think about" (Jackson 1998, 62). "The more we know about an object, the more we discover about its connections with other worldly things, the richer the meaning becomes" (Jackson 1998, 27). An experience changes the object experienced as well as the "experiencer."

Dewey and the Imagination

Dewey was a constructivist; learning is the process of building on prior experience and, through reflection, gaining new knowledge. And imagination enables new experiences to enter and connect with prior knowledge:

> For while the roots of every experience are found in the interaction of a live creature with its environment, that experience becomes conscious, a matter of perception, only when meanings enter it that are derived from prior experiences. Imagination is the only gateway through which these meanings can find their way into a present interaction; or rather, as we have just seen, the conscious adjustment of the new and the old is imagination. (Dewey 1934 [1959], 272).

Early in *Art as Experience,* Dewey quotes a lyrical passage from George Eliot's nineteenth-century novel *The Mill on the Floss* to illustrate the process:

> These familiar flowers, these well-remembered bird notes, this sky with its fitful brightness, these furrowed and grassy fields, each with a sort of personality given to it by the capricious hedge, such things as these are the mother tongue of our imagination, the language that is laden with all the subtle inextricable associations the fleeting hours of our childhood left behind them. Our delight in the sunshine on the deep-bladed grass today might be no more than the faint perception of wearied souls, if it were not for the sunshine and grass of far-off years, which still live in us and transform our perception into love (quoted in Dewey 1934 [1959], 18).

Although Kieran Egan and Dewey both place imagination at the center of learning, they talk about it in very different terms. Egan's view is the more elaborated, pragmatic, and prescriptive; it offers a clear methodology for liberating the learner's imaginative tools in service to knowledge acquisition.

Egan has incorporated one core tenet of constructivist educational theory: the idea of an active mind that creates knowledge. But he rejects the claim—central to constructivism—that learning must build on a foundation of prior knowledge. And despite his appeal to museum educators, Egan is not especially interested in the arts. Rather, he wants to help teachers and students master the basic course of study. His view of the imagination is thus highly instrumental and, in many ways, valuable to exhibition development—especially if one assumes that the goal of an exhibition is to transmit specific content. But if exhibitions exist to provide opportunities for imaginative play or meaning making—to whatever ultimate end—then Dewey's approach becomes useful not only because he has unlinked imagination from content acquisition, but also because the "conscious adjustment of the new and the old" seems an apt description of what visitors appear to actually be doing in exhibitions. For example, while the story of the young woman exploring Paul Revere's house (see chapter 3) might be analyzed in terms of different understandings and cognitive tools, on a fundamental level, it is about the ongoing process of integrating new and old through the imagination.[5]

Another vivid and delightful example of this process at work—what Mihaly Csikszentmihalyi might consider creativity—comes from one of the

Philadelphia Stories, told by an adult describing the actions of a youngster in a children's museum exhibition:

> [At the Madison Children's Museum], there's a dairy exhibit called *Cows, Curds and their Wheys*, and in that exhibit we have Holstein vests with udders on them that kids can put on. And one of the best things I ever saw was a little girl who had the vest with the udder on. And she was standing at the International Dairy Bar—which is part of this exhibit—with a glass from the dairy bar, trying to milk the cow vest into the glass, and then handing it to whoever was the patron at her dairy bar (M. Spock 1992, 6–7, 33–34; Spock and Leichter 1999, 77).[6]

One could certainly analyze this incident either in terms of imaginative education or child development theory or both. But it also illustrates Dewey's process: a visitor, in this case a young child, is drawing on what she is fleetingly familiar with—cows give milk, people drink from glasses, one stands at a bar—and putting it all together in her own unique way through the gateway of her imagination.[7]

Maxine Greene and Aesthetic Education

Among Dewey's many disciples is Maxine Greene, the distinguished professor emeritus of philosophy and education at Columbia University. Among Greene's several core principles, the idea that one must bring one's total self, one's lived life—reminiscent of Dewey's active mind—to the experience of works of art is paramount: "I do not believe that aesthetic contemplation or attending can take place apart from lived life" (Greene 2001, 40). Her philosophy informs every aspect of Lincoln Center Education (formerly the Lincoln Center Institute) where she was philosopher-in-residence. (She is thus unwittingly the person responsible for launching me on this inquiry.)

Greene is a fervent advocate of social justice and of the capacity for art to change lives. She shares Dewey's fundamental belief that "the moral function of art itself is to remove prejudice, do away with the scales that keep the eye from seeing, tear away the veils due to wont and custom, perfect the power to perceive" (quoted in Jackson 1998, 113). Works of art, she says, "have a potential for evoking an intimation of a better order of things, . . . a consciousness of possibility" (Greene 2001, 117). They can "nudge us out of somnolence and move us somehow to choose to act, to engage in a beginning" (121). Change must be imagined before it can be implemented, and thus "To learn, after all, is to become different, to see more, to gain a new perspective. It is to choose against things as they are" (1988, 45).

Greene's discussions of aesthetic agency employ brilliant language: art can "ward off chaos without denying it" and inspire "radical happiness" (Csikszentmihalyi 1997, 23). But we must bring our "lived" selves to the task; we must engage fully and passionately and openly. For those who do, art offers new possibilities, new ways of being. She quotes a line from Turgenev—"the ducks stand on tiptoe as the geese fly by"—that speaks metaphorically to the inspirational quality of works of art (Greene 2004).

Inevitably, Greene has thought deeply about the imagination. In a faculty seminar I attended at Bank Street College (2004), she identified three different kinds of imagination—poetic, ethical, and empathetic—and noted that our conventional understanding of imagination, derived largely from the romantics, is purely individualistic and thus in conflict with current sociocultural theory. This intriguing insight echoes current scholarship in many areas, including visitor studies—for example, the decision of the Minnesota History Center team that designed *Open House: If These Walls Could Talk* (see chapter 3) to look at conversations between visitors rather than the more traditional individual's experience. And it also mirrors Egan's socially constructed analysis of how imagination develops.

In my opinion, Greene is herself an artist; her materials are language and ideas. Like Egan, she is an outspoken critic of the current state of public education, which she believes gives far-too-short shrift to imagination and the arts, but she has little patience for what she might consider the prescriptive nature of imaginative education and no interest in using works of art to teach specific content.

Lincoln Center Institute has developed not standards for aesthetic education, but Capacities for Imaginative Learning that students could apply to different academic subjects as well as their own lives. These capacities include many of the habits of mind that surface throughout this book: noticing deeply, embodying, questioning, making connections, identifying patterns, exhibiting empathy, creating meaning, taking action, and reflecting/assessing.[8]

But while Lincoln Center chose to design a set of capacities and work closely with teachers in all content areas, they insist on beginning with the work of art itself—the experience itself, in Deweyian terms—not with whatever topics teachers may want to bring to it. The latter is brought in as contextual material after the learner has grappled with his or her own meaning making. Art and the aesthetic experience provide unique, complete, emotionally rich, and potentially transformative experiences in themselves. Thus, in examining, for instance, how Greene talks about the purpose and role of engaging the imagination, one perceives an opening up—an expansion of meaning, to use Dewey's term—that strikes a very different chord from Egan's more instrumental, content-driven approach. She writes:

> What has been encountered becomes an event within personal consciousness; it may begin shining toward the lived world. Clearly, we cannot *make* that happen; nor can we intrude when people are becoming aware in this way. We cannot grade them on whether or not such a phenomenon does occur. All we can do is to try and invent situations that make it more likely—allowing for time, for privacy, for silences. We have to try to move persons to *think about alternative ways of being alive, possible ways of inhabiting the world. And then we may be able to help them realize the sense in which an active imagination involves transactions between inner and outer vision* (Greene 2001, 32; emphasis added).

Mihaly Csikszentmihalyi and Happiness Through the Arts

In the 1990s, Lincoln Center Institute commissioned the psychologist Mihaly Csikszentmihalyi to comment on the results of a five-year study of its work with schools. Csikszentmihalyi is well known in museum education for his research on creativity and the theory of flow in learning. He also coauthored a book on the nature of aesthetic experience, *The Art of Seeing: An Interpretation of the Aesthetic Encounter* (1990), in which he likened the aesthetic experience to a "flow" experience, meaning there were feasible goals and intrinsic rewards for attaining them.

In his evaluation, "Assessing Aesthetic Education: Measuring the Ability to 'Ward Off Chaos'" (1997), Csikszentmihalyi laments the practice of using cognitive tools, developed for standard subject matter, to assess the impact of aesthetic learning. In language recalling Egan's history of imagination as being viewed as inferior to reason, he says the arts have been marginalized as mere leisure activities, unsuited to knowledge acquisition. Trying to justify them on purely cognitive grounds is a futile enterprise based on a misunderstanding of "the essence of what the arts are about."

Quoting Maxine Greene above, he writes that art "gives us a taste of 'radical happiness'" and teaches how to "ward off chaos without denying it." Happiness is and has always been the "highest goal of human life and happiness cannot be achieved through material means" but rather "depends on the quality of subjective experience, which in turn depends on a person's ability to control his or her consciousness, . . . taking neutral or negative objective conditions, and transforming them into positive subjective experiences" (Csikszentmihalyi 1997, 6).

Csikszentmihalyi describes four major dimensions to aesthetic experience:

- The sensory—the pleasure art brings our eyes, ears, and physical bodies;
- The emotional—"feelings of awe, wonder, delight, fear, or relief that break through the gray affectless daily routines and expand the range of what it means to be alive";
- The cognitive, which involve thought and understanding; and
- The transcendent, which "involves the very real feeling we have after an aesthetic encounter that some kind of growth has taken place, that our being and the cosmos have been realigned in a more harmonious way" (Csikszentmihalyi 1997, 25).

Ultimately, he argues, we need to "emancipate aesthetic education from its dependence on cognitive results, and begin defending it on grounds that are more congruent with its essence" (Csikszentmihalyi 1997, 25). Since the essence of aesthetic education is its contribution to human happiness, we should try to design assessments that demonstrate its impact not only on students of aesthetic education but also and ultimately on the long-term "quality of life as a whole."

Dewey's ideas invite us to think about exhibitions as aesthetic experiences, possibly even as art itself—depending on how we define art and which of his principles apply. His "both-and" continuum way of thinking is liberating but also challenging. There is no clear line between, for example, the sunset and the painting. Greene's and Csikszentmihalyi's focus, on the other hand, is squarely on works of art as we usually understand the term: literature, painting and sculpture, film, and the performing arts. And certainly Jackson, in interpreting Dewey, draws a critical distinction between aesthetic experience centered on works of art and aesthetic experience that occurs in other ways. Not one of them talks about exhibitions—including exhibitions of works of art. Were they not familiar with or interested in them, because exhibitions were assumed to do something other than offer an aesthetic experience, like teaching content? Or had they simply never thought about them? I am guessing the latter is true.[9]

The challenge is finding an appropriate place for exhibitions on the continuum of "both-and." Some include works of art, while others are curated or designed by acknowledged artists. But drawing on Dewey—and more recent interpretations such as Latham's discussion of numinous encounters with objects—*all* exhibitions have the potential to be aesthetic, even if they do not formally contain works of art. To borrow Csikszentmihalyi's language, to what extent might exhibitions be about "sensations, feelings, and meanings" rather than "reasoning and knowing" (Csikszentmihalyi 1997, 25)? And do any or all of the four dimensions—sensory, emotional, cognitive, and transcendent—apply? Can an exhibition provide *an* experience—one that in Dewey's terms truly runs its course and in Csikszentmihalyi's evokes all these dimensions—or is it more likely to offer a series of discrete experiences, each of which may or may not be aesthetic? Does the ultimate dimension of "transcendence"—which Csikszentmihalyi defines as "the very real feeling we have after an aesthetic encounter that some kind of growth has taken place; that our being and the cosmos have been re-aligned in a more harmonious way" (Csikszentmihalyi 1997, 7)—have any relevance to a medium that is at root about sharing knowledge? Or might we, as Csikszentmihalyi urged the Lincoln Center Institute to do, look beyond "reasoning and knowing" (page 25 of same article above) and think about something as "elusive but essential as human happiness"?

Conceptualizing exhibitions as aesthetic experience—as a kind of art in the lower case—asks museum professionals to contemplate different goals and different standards for evaluation. And that, in turn, demands a different way of working, which I will address in my final chapter.

PART THREE

Working in the Subjunctive Mood

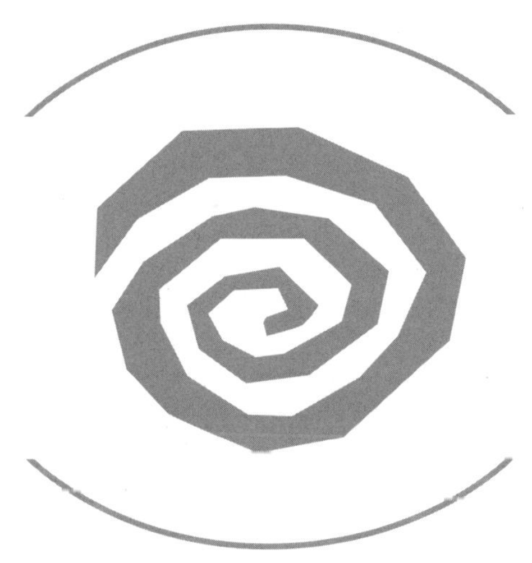

CHAPTER 6

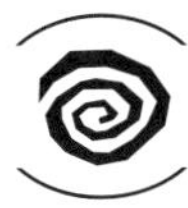

Creating and Experiencing the Exhibition Medium

> There's a milk can at the Holocaust Museum [in Washington, D.C.]. It's real. Where people in the Warsaw Ghetto hid records about themselves, scribbled on little pieces of paper, as a way of making a mark. And there is this milk can. And it's just tremendously evocative (M. Spock 1992, 44–08).

In 1973, visitor studies pioneer Harris Shettel published an often-cited piece called "Exhibits: Art Form or Educational Medium?" In those early and still tentative days of visitor studies and formal evaluation, he was eager to convince the museum field that "exhibits *can* be considered an educational medium, and they are therefore subject to all the same basic laws and principles that would apply to any other educational medium" (Shettel 1973, 39). Behind his argument is a long history of disagreement between those who saw the mission of museums as aesthetic and those who insisted it was educational, a divide that has come to stand for a focus on content over learner, on initiated and elite over the general public, on expert over beginner. Just as the difference of opinion between such historical figures as Benjamin Ives Gilman and George Brown Goode has been exaggerated in museum writings (see chapter 1), today we can overstate disagreements between, for instance, curators and educators. The line blurs as museums continue to acknowledge a visitor-centered mission and practice, and the possibilities for genuine, visitor-centered collaboration proliferate.[1]

Leslie Bedford, "Creating and Experiencing the Exhibition Medium" in *The Art of Museum Exhibitions: How Story and Imagination Create Aesthetic Experiences*. pp. 91–128.

I am not interested in resurrecting an old argument with its either-or language. Exhibitions are both education and art, and we can think about them from numerous perspectives. To reframe the conversation and see exhibitions as the unique medium they are requires using old language in new ways, bringing the imagination back to center stage. We must ask ourselves what it would mean to see exhibitions as aesthetic experiences, with imagining—an active process, not a static noun—as the main activity. What would it look like to work in the subjunctive mood?

One might begin by examining the process for developing exhibitions, which is so critical to their success. What are the different roles on an exhibition team, and what skills and constructs does each involve? This is the approach of Polly McKenna-Cress and Janet Kamien, whose book, *Creating Exhibitions: Collaboration in the Planning, Development, and Design of Innovative Experiences* (2013) is brilliantly organized by advocacy: for the institution, for the subject matter, for visitor experiences, for design, for the project and the team. But mine is not a book about how to make exhibitions. Rather, it is about the habits of mind that every member of the team, regardless of task, should adopt if she wants to create an aesthetic experience for visitors.[2]

What follows is an attempt to apply the ideas inherent in my three "tent poles"—story, imagination, and aesthetic experience—to creating and experiencing the exhibition medium. Although I have pulled these ideas apart in this chapter, they are inevitably and deeply connected.

Objects Help Visitors Create Their Own Narratives

Objects—Botticelli's *Venus*, Daniel Boone's gun, the Book of Kells, Lincoln's hat, and many things less memorable—are what museums "collect, preserve, and display," as they trumpeted in their mission statements before they shifted to visitor and community engagement. But while reverence for the object may be muted in favor of making a difference to society at large, objects remain what distinguishes museums from other cultural institutions. They have the concrete evidence of human culture over time and place.

But how we think about objects' roles in exhibitions has changed. From sacred centerpieces to punctuations for narratives to stage props, objects have undergone the postmodern transformation: personal interpretation is all. In fact, treating objects as separate reality unmoored from human interpretation is a waste of time. Spencer Crew and James Sims, who created the Smithsonian exhibition *Field to Factory* (see chapter 2), argue that "the problem with things is that they are dumb. They are not eloquent, as some thinkers in art museums claim. They are dumb. And if by some ventriloquism they seem to speak, they lie" (Crew and Sims 1991, 159).

Crew and Sims were addressing the issue of authenticity, a criterion more important for scholars and museum professionals than for the general public. They wanted readers to understand that in crafting the twentieth-century metanarrative of the African American migration north, they basically created a stage set where objects were often chosen for their narrative power rather than their authenticity. The collections of the National Museum of American History, like most, were built over time by people whose choices reflected their personal, cultural, and historical biases. So if the goal is to create a narrative—and thus an experience—the design team's choices are inevitably subjective on several levels. In other words, as Crew and Sims write, "authenticity is not about factuality or reality. It is about authority. Objects have no authority; people do" (Crew and Sims 1991, 163).

Unbound by institutional or professional concern for the historical record, the visitor is entirely free to respond to objects as she pleases. Since story generates story, she creates her own narrative of the exhibition's narrative and associates with objects along the path in whatever way she pleases. As these layers of meaning making accrue over time like layers of wallpaper in an old house, the concept of *authentic* in the classic sense dissolves into air.

John Dewey had little patience for those who revered the authentic for its own sake, in part because it implied an elitist aestheticism. His criterion for judging the value of an object was whether it engendered an aesthetic experience, and not if it was an original or a copy of one. I believe that the real thing provides an important contribution to exhibition as aesthetic experience. It just may be that its "realness" is in the eye of the beholder.

This short story from the Philadelphia collection is one of many that, like the story about Babe Ruth's bat in chapter 4, speaks to the power of the authentic object:

> My first recollection of a museum . . . was in South Dakota—I believe a Buffalo Bill museum. And I remember seeing a scalp and seeing a tomahawk, and suddenly understanding as a youngster, this was real hair, this was a real weapon (M. Spock 1992, 4.7).

At the same time, it appears that something doesn't have to be the real thing—in the sense of original or authentic—to generate strong reactions. For instance, one visitor to *Choosing to Participate* told me at great length how moved she had been by the dress Elizabeth Eckford wore the morning she tried to enter Central High School (see fig. 1). But it wasn't her real dress; it was a copy sewn by the exhibit designer's mother, one of several props. The visitor may have assumed it *was* the original, or perhaps its power came from something else: the context of Elizabeth's recreated teen's bedroom with 1950s music in the background (also made up), the universality of getting ready for the first day at a new school, or perhaps the visitor's memories of the iconic photographs published in *Life* magazine of Elizabeth in her real dress. I don't know, but I do know that in our digital age, the notion of the real thing is harder and harder to pin down.

Kiersten Latham is trying. But what she is looking for is language that comes from visitors, not professionals. Her research (2013) suggests four ways people think about the "realness" of museum objects:

- Real means original or authentic;
- Everything is real, but some things are "special";
- Real is contextual, environmental, or participatory; and
- Real is "what you think it is."

In any case, it seems our concern with authenticity is limited and not terribly useful if we are thinking in terms of the visitor experience. Rather, the meaning of authentic or real emerges from the nature and quality of the interactive experience between exhibit maker, object, and visitor. Both Daniel Boone's gun and Elizabeth Eckford's dress coexist in the imagined world created simultaneously by design team and visitor.[3]

Metaphor Stirs the Imagination to Generate Meaning

Metaphor is the kind of term that crops up in literary criticism and academic circles and tends to turn practitioners off.[4] But it is relevant to working in the subjunctive mood and visitor-centered practice. Metaphor involves talking about something in terms derived from something very different. By generating, not simply articulating, relationships among disparate things or ideas, metaphor expands our understanding. Thus, for Kieran Egan, it is a significant cognitive tool. As he puts it in *A Very Short History of the Imagination*, "If the mood of the imagination is the subjunctive, its trope is metaphor" (Egan 2007, 14). Interestingly, metaphor is most evident in very young children and then begins to atrophy at age eight or nine, when literacy begins. Its disappearance over the lifespan is a loss, he says, not a gain.

Jerome Bruner writes about metaphor in literary discourse as one of several strategies writers use to recruit the reader's imagination or "subjunctivize" reality. By this he means putting the reader in the mode of "trafficking in human possibilities rather than in settled certainties" (Bruner 1986, 26). In his felicitous phrase, metaphor "evokes zestful imaginative play" (Bruner 1986, 4).

Probably the best-known use of object as metaphor in the museum exhibitions in the United States is Fred Wilson's extraordinary *Mining the Museum* at the Maryland Historical Society in 1992.[5] Asked to rummage through the society's collections and bring to light whatever caught his eye, Wilson created powerful metaphors for the African American experience. The installation most often cited is the case displaying a pair of metal slave shackles juxtaposed with an elegant silver tea service.[6]

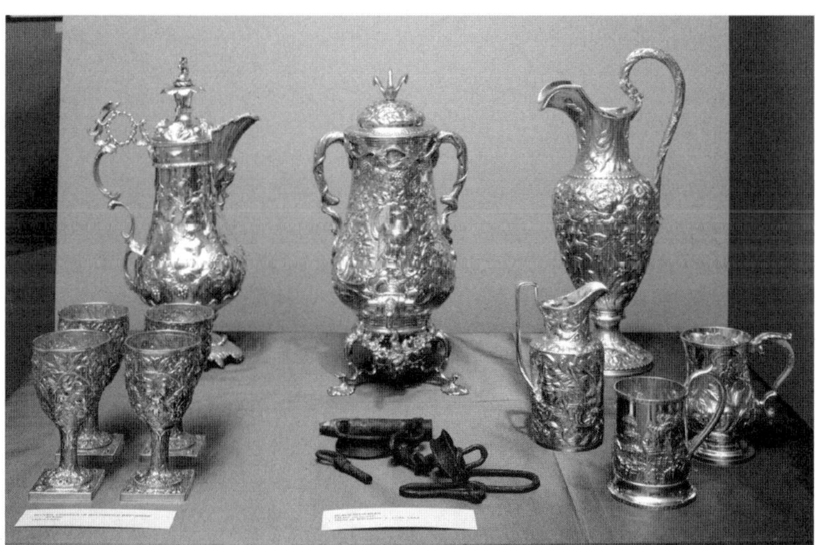

"Metalwork," artist Fred Wilson's installation of slave shackles juxtaposed with an elaborate silver tea service, was one of the most memorable parts of *Mining the Museum*. Courtesy of the Maryland Historical Society, Item ID # MTM010.

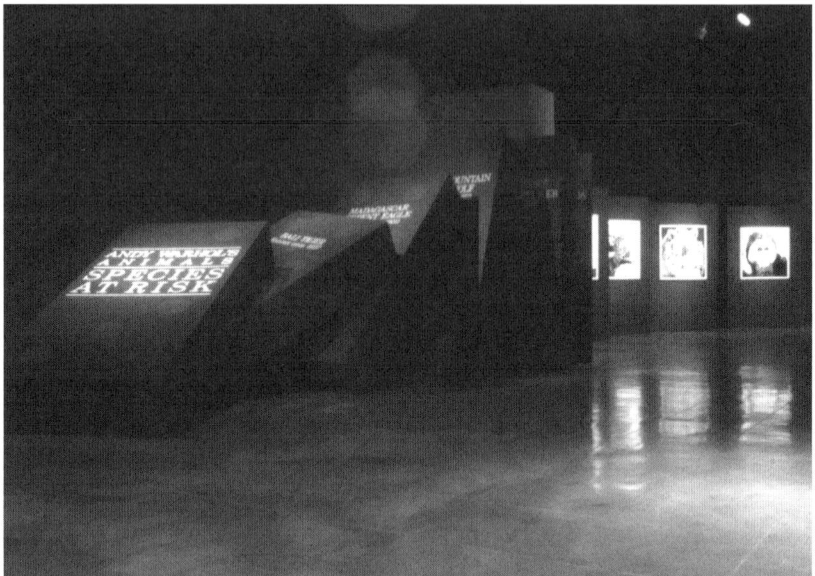

Designer Don Hughes created a collapsing set of giant dominoes for the entrance to *Warhol's Animals: Species at Risk* at the San Diego Museum of Natural History. Photo courtesy of Don Hughes.

Artists and designers often work with metaphor. François Confino, an artist-designer much admired by his peers, created several memorable exhibitions at the Natural History Museum of Los Angeles in the early 2000s. In *L.A.: light/motion/dreams*, for example, he placed a coyote on the diving board of a backyard pool to express the disappearing boundary between nature and the built environment. In 1983, exhibition designer Don Hughes used the metaphor of a collapsing row of giant dominos to introduce the exhibition *Warhol's Animals: Species at Risk* at the San Diego Museum of Natural History. The permanent exhibition at the United States Holocaust Memorial Museum unfolds as a cinema-like narrative punctuated by a number of memorable metaphorical uses of collections materials. The thousands of shoes left by Jewish victims as they entered the gas chambers is probably the most vivid and horrific, and visitors often say they are the most intense memory they have of the exhibition.

Displays like these apparently work metaphorically for many people. They are always cited, at least by museum colleagues, as among their most powerful experiences. Metaphor can express and evoke possibility, the "what-if?" open-ended interpretation and expansive creation of meaning that characterizes the aesthetic experience. While adults may be less comfortable than young children in making metaphor, they are still capable of responding to its generative energy, especially—perhaps only—when the metaphor is accessible.

Metaphor is thus one of several ways of stirring the imagination to generate meaning, or, as Dewey would say, of creating an expansion of meaning. To illustrate this key concept, Philip W. Jackson uses a simple teaspoon to explain how objects can evoke either intrinsic meaning, which is expressive and enjoyed for its own sake ("its luster and its shape, the simplicity of its lines, the balanced feel of holding it"), or extrinsic meaning, which is instrumental (its use in cracking an egg or stirring one's coffee). He points out that a meaning can be experienced both intrinsically and extrinsically:

> When I gaze at the spoon and thrill at the thought that Queen Victoria may have stirred her tea with it, just as I am using it now for my coffee, its historical meaning is being expressively undergone. If, however, I make use of that same knowledge to bolster a historical argument of some kind, I am treating it instrumentally. I could conceivably be doing both at the same time (Jackson 2000, 31).

Intrinsic meaning is indubitably characteristic of art-centered experience and it is not foreign to non-art exhibitions. Many of the Philadelphia Stories are about artifacts, not art objects, and most express intrinsic meanings:

> My favorite object in all of the museum world is at the Henry Ford Museum in Michigan. . . . And that's a test tube with Thomas Alva Edison's last breath in it. Now that has got to be the most incredible object that any museum has. I mean, I can't think of anything that would surpass that (M. Spock 1992, 9.10; 2000b, 17).

But other evidence of objects, like Jackson's spoon, generate both:

> My first museum memory was the color wheels, the really large color wheels at one of the art museums in New York City that were kid-size so that you could stand right up to it. They're probably as big as me. And you could just spin colors that were transparencies. Nothing fancy. But it made me understand how mixing colors did things, and how beautiful certain colors were next to one another; I love it (M. Spock 1992, 9.13).

In the exhibition *Vietnam: Journeys of Mind, Body and Spirit* at the American Museum of Natural History in New York City in 2003–2004,[7] an elegant glass case held an open, empty ceramic box accompanied by a small container of incense and a vase of flowers. I learned that the box was a coffin, used in the north to house the retrieved and cleaned bones of deceased family members and to provide a final resting place for their souls. The text read:

> **Wandering Ghosts**
>
> *Unhappy Spirits of the Dead*
>
> Wandering ghosts are the unhappy spirits of people who died too young, whose deaths were violent or unexpected, or who died far from home without a proper burial by their families. The need to bring home those who have died far away and to bury them properly is deeply felt. Failure at this task is far more than a bitter personal loss; it condemns the loved one to wander the Earth restlessly for eternity.
>
> Out of pity, people make offerings of food, paper money and clothing to these wandering ghosts throughout the year, especially on the fifteenth day of the seventh lunar month, when all souls are freed from hell for a day.
>
> This space is an offering to all wandering ghosts, military and civilian, Vietnamese and foreign, who lost their lives in the armed struggles and wars that engulfed Vietnam in the 20th century.

For me, the display engendered a meditation on life and death, on my generation and the futility of war, on cross-cultural understanding or the lack thereof, and many, many other things. I have often revisited it in my memory, where it continues to stir my imagination. In fact, it illustrates many of the ideas raised in earlier chapters: it had resonance, was numinous, and involved perception rather than mere recognition. However, for someone of another generation, gender, or way of thinking, this same artful arrangement of open box, flowers, incense, and bilingual poetic text could stimulate other but presumably equally expansive meanings. That they are different is less significant to this discussion than that they occur.

Uniqueness Is the Gateway to Story and Imagination

Dewey says over and over that the "*product* of art . . . is not the *work* of art," but rather the nature of the interaction between the work and the human being who experiences it (1934, 214).[8] The qualities of this interaction cannot be subdivided and analyzed because they adhere to the particular experience itself. As he says, "no two sunsets have exactly the same red" (215). The particular red of a particular sunset informs the aesthetic experience with it. The potential for meaningful experience, therefore, lies not in the so-called universal but in the specific, the concrete, the particular detail that can, in some circumstances, become the inspiration for what might be called the universality of emotional response.

In 2004 the distinguished stage actress Kathleen Chalfant performed a one-person play called *The Letter* at the Lucille Lortell Theatre in New York. Portraying a Jewish Socialist doctor incarcerated by the Nazis, she pours out her fear of dying in a letter to her son. As we later learn, the letter was real; the son received it along with news of her death. It is a heartbreaking performance both because of her artistry and because, as she later said (and I paraphrase): We can only understand an event like the Holocaust through a single story of an individual. In analyzing the qualities of great literature, Bruner says "it strives to put its timeless miracles into the particulars of experience, and to locate the experience in time and place. Joyce thought of the particularities of the story as epiphanies of the ordinary" (Bruner 1986, 13).

Bernice Johnson Reagon, founder of the singing group Sweet Honey in the Rock, said something similar: "One of the things I've learned from being in Sweet Honey. . . is that when you are as specific as you can be about who you are, you are the most universal." Describing a song she wrote about her own grandmother, she says:

> We'd be singing it, and I'd see white people in the audience crying. . . . And I would think, what is it they're understanding? Because in the song I'm saying, "I never knew that my nose was too flat, I never knew that my skin was too black." So I'm thinking, literally, what is it about this that they get? But they had comparable experiences, and somebody in their family loved them unconditionally and let them know they were special (quoted in Toumani 2005).

The ability of the unique moment, person, or story to evoke an entire universe is a quality of an aesthetic experience in any medium, including exhibitions. The founders of the United States Holocaust Memorial Museum understood this well. The exhibition weaves the specific detail—Chalfant's point—within the bigger stories. One of the many powerful experiences there is the Tower of Faces, the three-story room walled by individual photographs of thousands of Lithuanian villagers killed by the Nazis. The abstraction of mass murder is brought to life by the specificity of individual faces.

The Philadelphia Stories yield an interesting memory of an encounter with a small brush hair embedded in a painting that enabled the visitor to imagine Rubens' hand at work:

> There's one other experience that I think about and that's a particular Rubens painting at the Norton Simon Museum in Pasadena. It's a pretty crappy painting, actually. But what's interesting to me about it is that sort of halfway up on the right side, there's a hair imbedded in the paint, just a hair from the brush. It's just sticking out of the paint. And I don't care about the painting, or what it's about . . . . What interested me was that, at a particular moment in time, when the hair was connected to the brush that was connected to the hand . . . . There was a particular moment when that hair came out and it stuck in the painting and it . . . had come from Rubens' hand. . . . And so that, wherever you can, when you can reveal that moment, I guess that's what's the most interesting to me (M. Spock 1992, 17.9).

Turning to a more monumental example of the specific, the central atrium of the National Underground Railroad Freedom Center in Cincinnati holds an extraordinary artifact: a slave pen, found in Kentucky, that had been used to hold up to 75 slaves who were being moved to the South. All cleaned up and empty, it sits alone in the gleaming lobby. The enclosure had been completely denuded of any physical presence, rendered almost mute. At the time I visited, visitors could only enter with a guide who pointed out what to notice: up high on a rafter were the remains of a metal loop to which slaves would have been chained. That small artifact—that concrete detail—gave me at least whatever resonance the installation possesses.[9]

The transcripts from the *Open House* exhibition are full of examples of visitors connecting with the meaning of the exhibition through the concrete details of individual lives. For instance, numerous visitors remarked on the story of Henrietta Schumacher, who wasted away from "sugar sickness," today's diabetes, in the early 1890s. In this conversation, a 46-year-old woman (F1) and a 51-year-old woman (F2) stand in the first room—the Schumachers' parlor—where they have discovered her portrait and that bit of information. They express amazement (what Daniel Spock calls wonderment) and empathy:

F1: Uhuh, you just, uhuh . . . . Oh . . . . Every morning, five o'clock . . . . Oh my god! . . . . Oh, did you know that? . . . Did you read this?

F2: Yeah, I read it.

F1: Did you know that?

F2: No.

F1: I didn't either. My goodness . . . .

F2: Starvation . . . .

F1: Oh . . . they only get as much food . . . .

F2: Because they were the minimal amount your body could handle. Just to keep you alive. Barely alive . . . .

F1: Oh . . . .

F2: Uhuh.

F1: It'd be awful to have diabetes, wouldn't it? (Ellenbogen et al. 2006a, 40).

In *The Museum Experience Revisited*, John Falk and Lynn Dierking analyze how visitors respond to objects in exhibitions. At first they are attracted to the biggest and most valuable, but then they look for the familiar because, they suggest, people are attracted to what they already sort of know about and find interesting. They don't respond to objects as illustrations of abstract ideas—the big ideas that animate the exhibition makers—but rather on the more superficial, concrete level of: What is it? Where does it come from? What is it used for? (Falk and Dierking 2012, 111) The *Open House* example, among many others, suggests that the concrete—and the familiar—can become the gateway to imagination and story.

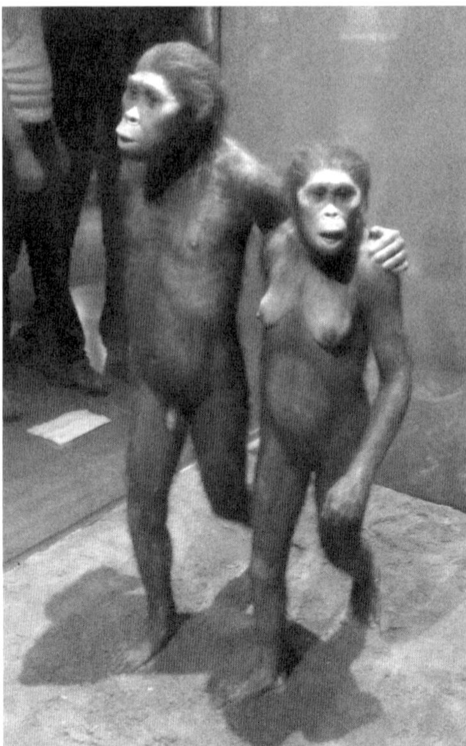

A close-up of "Lucy and Desi," the iconic figures from the Hall of Human Origins at the American Museum of Natural History. Photo courtesy of Richard Cress.

Narrativity Inspires Internal Conversations

In chapter 3, I referred to narrativity, a literary term that describes the power to evoke story in the listener's or viewer's mind. As suggested earlier, something does not have to be a formal story (with setting, action, and characters) in order to generate one. And the generation of story is, like every aspect of exhibitions discussed so far, highly subjective.

According to anecdotal evidence from museum staff, one of the most popular installations at the American Museum of Natural History was *Australopithecus afarensis*, known as "Lucy," in the Hall of Human Biology and Evolution. Naturalist and writer Diane Ackerman has provided an unforgettable description of her personal encounter with Lucy and her mate in *A Natural History of Love* (1994) that illustrates the power of narrativity to evoke not only story, but, by extension, Dewey's expansion of meaning:

> A volcanic eruption, shown in the background, is coating the landscape with white ash and as they walk through the savanna, they leave a trail of footprints. Lucy's head is turned left, her mouth open. She seems startled by us. She does not know what she will become. Looking forward as he walks, her mate has his arm around her shoulder in a familiar gesture of tenderness. She doesn't know about dinner dates, Valentine's Day, custody battles. What was their courtship like? What worries them? Do they imagine a future? What delights their senses? How do they comfort their young? I long to meet them face-to-face, to reach through time and touch them. It is like recognizing one's kin across the street in a bustling city" (Ackerman 1994, 335).

In 2007, the museum opened a new Hall of Human Origins and updated the presentation. Fortunately, scientific evidence still supported the storyline of two figures, one larger than the other, walking together across the plains: two sets of footprints had been preserved in the volcanic ash for some three million years. But the museum dispensed with the rather fanciful backdrop and installed the figures at ground level. It is perhaps harder—for an adult though not necessarily for children—to empathize with these quite short (and more simian) figures, but their pose remains evocative and replete with narrativity. The installation thus meets criteria both of scientific truth and artistic authenticity.

In contrast, there is *Australopithecus afarensis* in the National Museum of Anthropology in Mexico City. This Lucy stands upright and alone in her display case, a humanlike creature hirsute but clearly female. Lacking any contextual details of setting or companion, there is no way to make the kinds of personal connections Ackerman, or anyone less fanciful, might make, no way to find story as the youngster looking at the jaguar diorama did (see chapter 2). The museum appears to have little interest in engaging the visitor's imagination and virtually none in creating any kind of aesthetic experience. Rather, the intention—as is most typical in the museum field—is to transmit information visually and through text.

The "Lucy and Desi" display in the American Museum of Natural History—as the staff nicknamed it—raises another question about storytelling in exhibitions. Are some kinds of stories more likely to engage people than others? What might exhibitions do to make the process of personal story making more active?

I suspect that the narrative that Lucy and her mate suggested to Ackerman and to me as well—a couple setting off on their life's journey together—is one of those primal stories that crosses barriers of culture and gender. In designing an exhibition, might the team consider the effects such universal stories can have on their visitors? To my knowledge, few exhibitions do this intentionally, with the exception of Noah's Ark in Los Angeles, discussed later in this chapter. But the creators of an excellent program for young people at the Centre for New Enlightenment in Glasgow's Kelvingrove Art Gallery and Museum did. Designed to build "self-belief," it draws quite deliberately on the Jungian archetypes depicted in Joseph Campbell's monumental study, *The Hero with a Thousand Faces,* to design a set of personal challenges or quests for early adolescents. The program reflects not only the museum's commitment to its community but its choice of story as the main interpretive strategy for the entire institution.[10]

In any case, it is undeniable that regardless of the exhibition maker's intention, visitors will use their imaginations to reinterpret the story presented according to personal experience, as well as whatever master plots they may bring to it.

Written text, of course, is the usual way to tell a story in an exhibition. Two examples of object labels from quite different settings contain equally high levels of narrativity. The first accompanies a fourth-century B.C. Phoenician sarcophagus at the Beirut National Museum:

> In this coffin lie I, Batnoam, mother of King Ozbaal, king of Byblos, son of Paltibaal, priest of the lady, in a robe and with a tiara on my head, and a gold leaf on my mouth, as was the custom with the royal ladies who were before me.

The second example is from a collection of photographs exhibited at the Center for Jewish History in New York City called *And I Still See Their Faces: Images of Polish Jews:*

> I carried this photograph of my mama through two selections by Dr. Mengele at Auschwitz. Once, I held it in my mouth, the second time, I had it taped with a bandage to the bottom of my foot. I was 14 years old.
>
> My dear mama, daddy, little sister Gizia and brother Abrahamek were already dead. They hid in the Plaszów camp to avoid the deportation to Auschwitz. The commandant of the camp discovered them on March 24, 1943 and shot them on the spot.
>
> *Zahava Bromberg, Tel Aviv*

The second example tells a story directly, and the first does not. But both illustrate how narrativity can be enhanced by paying attention to both imaginative education and brain research. Kieran Egan urges educators to use vivid language to create images in their students' minds—a conceptual tool associated with the acquisition and mastery of literacy or Romantic understanding. Brain research contributes an understanding of how particular language works through mirror neurons. Science writer Annie Murphy Paul (2012) explains how language rich in sensory associations—lavender, cinnamon, leathery hands, or a velvety voice—light up the olfactory or sensory cortex just the way actual experience with these phenomena does. In other words, brain research suggests that in encountering pictorial and sensory language such as "a gold leaf in my mouth" or "taped to the bottom of my foot"—language that evokes an emotional response—the reader or the museum visitor is more apt to pay attention, feel, and perhaps remember the experience. Thus one senses the gold leaf in the mouth, the tiara on the head, the photograph taped to the bottom of a foot, and is completely there in the experience.[11]

Of course, sensory-rich language can be spoken as well as written. A few years ago I went on a tour of a re-created apartment at the Lower East Side Tenement Museum in Manhattan. The Irish-American family who lived there was wretchedly poor; the cost of a funeral for their youngest child eventually forced them to seek even cheaper living quarters. The educator-guide, an actor, began the experience by describing the neighborhood in the 1860s and then, reaching down to lift imaginary skirts, said, "Come. Let us pick our way through the garbage and horse carcasses and travel back in time." Her vividly descriptive language—as well as her familiar gesture—helped me connect with this long-ago place and time.

Voice is another aspect of text and thus a shaper of the experience. The classic voice in museums is third person, usually the curator's. First-person narration is less common. In the Little Rock section of *Choosing to Participate*, the design team recorded the adult Elizabeth Eckford recalling the day she tried to enter Central High School. Her voice, although an adult interpretation of a distant though still very painful memory, forges an emotional connection to her adolescent experience in a way that a third-person interpretation could not. It is not surprising that filmmaker Ken Burns chooses so often to use first-person voice, often in the form of letters, rather than the typical documentary talking head to create narrative and emotional engagement. First person is, after all, the voice of the storyteller.

At the National September 11 Memorial Museum, the voices of witnesses will be central to the experience. A gallery called *We Remember* provides a place for visitors to contribute their personal stories to an ongoing database that will infuse the entrance to the museum with voices from around the world. Jake Barton—principal of Local Projects, the firm that designed the oral history project StoryCorps—spoke in a TED talk called "The Museum of You" about his team's desire to create an "institution as listening experience" (Barton 2013).

Research supports the importance of first person over third. In her essay, "Write and Design with the Family in Mind," exhibit planner and writer Judy Rand says that researchers at the USS *Constitution* Museum found that visitors preferred first-person to third-person voice in exhibition labels by a margin of almost two to one (Rand 2010, 267).

Bur third person can still have narrativity, as it does in this example from a New York State Museum exhibition called *Lost Cases, Recovered Lives: Suitcases from a State Hospital Attic.* The label text is about Ethel S., one of the twelve patients at Willard State Hospital who are profiled in the exhibition. Ethel lived at Willard for forty-three years until her death in 1973.

> Ethel was the daughter of a Methodist minister. As a child growing up in Ithaca, she sang and played the piano and was active in church. When she was 18, she married a plumber named Seymour, and they soon had two children—a son in 1909 and a daughter in 1911. Seymour drank too much, flew into violent rages, and had affairs with other women. Ethel suffered a miscarriage, but then bore two more children, both of whom died as infants.
>
> After she left Seymour, Ethel continued to support herself by sewing for her neighbors. In 1930, her divorce final, she was admitted to Willard. Her file states: "She refused to leave the place where she was living and went to bed saying she was ill. . . . As she refused to leave the house, the landlady made a petition for her commitment."
>
> At certain times, Ethel appeared to be content at Willard and believed that the staff could help cure her ailment. . . . At other times, Ethel proved to be sarcastic and irritable, and she refused to do any work but crocheting. She did like to read. From 1930 to 1940, her children visited her three times. After 1940, they never came to see her at all. In her 43 years at Willard, Ethel never received any psychiatric

> medications. She died at the state hospital on June 12, 1973, at the age of 82.
>
> The wooden case accompanying Ethel S.'s story contained crocheted baby caps and gowns along with quilts and tableware (quoted in Bedford 2005, 217).

This text is so long that one might assume it would shut down the visitor's imagination. But this does not happen, in my opinion, for two reasons: it reads as a story, and it doesn't tell you what to think. Rather, you are left to muse on the possible meanings. I found myself wondering why Ethel's children didn't visit her for thirty years. Was she impossible to be with? Were they ashamed of her? Were there grandchildren she never saw? What happened to make a family behave like that? And then, for me, the thought: Who am I to judge? The exhibition provides the facts but then lets the visitor construct her own meanings (Bedford 2005).

The text is similar to the kind that the director of the United Stated Holocaust Memorial Museum insisted on using in the permanent exhibition, recalls Elaine Heumann Gurian, the museum's deputy director at the time. Trained in film, Jeshajahu Weinberg went through the exhibition script deleting any language that told the visitor how to feel or think (Gurian 2000). He was ensuring that there would be an internal conversation between the visitor and his imagination.

The idea that less can be more in writing exhibition text is problematic. In recent decades, museums, especially art museums, have been criticized for failing to give visitors enough information in terms they can understand. When Crew and Sims called objects "dumb," they were undermining the classic curatorial claim that objects should be left to speak for themselves. This perspective is rarely invoked these days when museums of all sorts have adopted a host of strategies for helping ordinary people "hear" what the objects are saying.[12]

But I am talking about something else: the phenomenon, all too common, of telling visitors everything there is to know about a topic or an object rather than assuming that they can, and will, decide for themselves—if they stick around long enough to pay attention. For example, one needn't be told that life at Willard State Hospital was hard for Ethel S. The information that her family only came three times in thirty years, and that she spent her days crocheting the baby clothes that are now displayed, allows us to employ our empathic imaginations and create our own understanding of her state of mind.

Embodied Experiences Engage All the Senses

Falk and Dierking conclude that museum visitors "devote most of their time to looking, touching, smelling and listening—not to reading (2012, 113).[13] Nonetheless, reading is what we mostly ask visitors to do, and throughout an exhibition, the visual is the main sense we employ. Imaginative education and cognitive studies—as well as visitor studies data and the field's growing interest in accessibility and multiple modalities for learning—suggest we should broaden the sensory palate and take advantage of the benefits of a rich interaction among our various senses. One often employed is hearing.

Several Philadelphia Stories recall memories of the iconic walkthrough *Giant Heart* at Philadelphia's Franklin Institute, where sound plays a role in sparking the imagination:

> The beating heart at the Franklin Institute when I was a kid. I think I went there when I was probably eight years old. And that experience that I remember much more distinctly and vividly than I think it really occurred, where there's this pounding, and you're going through a heart, and you're seeing how things might travel, and you get a really different perspective. I loved changing perspective, and to be able to feel like you were a blood cell going through, and it was great (M. Spock 1992, 9.13; 1999b, 10).[14]

In the 1990s, the Field Museum in Chicago installed an ambitious exhibition called *Life Over Time* that sought to teach visitors everything known about the beginnings of life on earth, employing multiple strategies for communicating such essentially incomprehensible concepts as "a billion years ago." One delightful bit was a chance to hear how an *apatosaurus* (also known as *brontosaurus*) would have sounded lumbering across the primordial swamps. Woofers mimicked the noise that an animal the size of four elephants would make, and the floor shook (Bedford 2012, 398).

Elaborate soundscapes increase the immersive nature of many exhibitions. One of the more sophisticated, at least for its time, is the permanent exhibition at Connecticut's Mashantucket Pequot Museum and Research Center. Passing through the moving narrative of the Pequots' environment before their first (and disastrous) encounters with Europeans in the late seventeenth century—a series of freestanding life-size dioramas—one hears dense layers of bird song, human voices, wind in the trees, wild animals, and other sounds

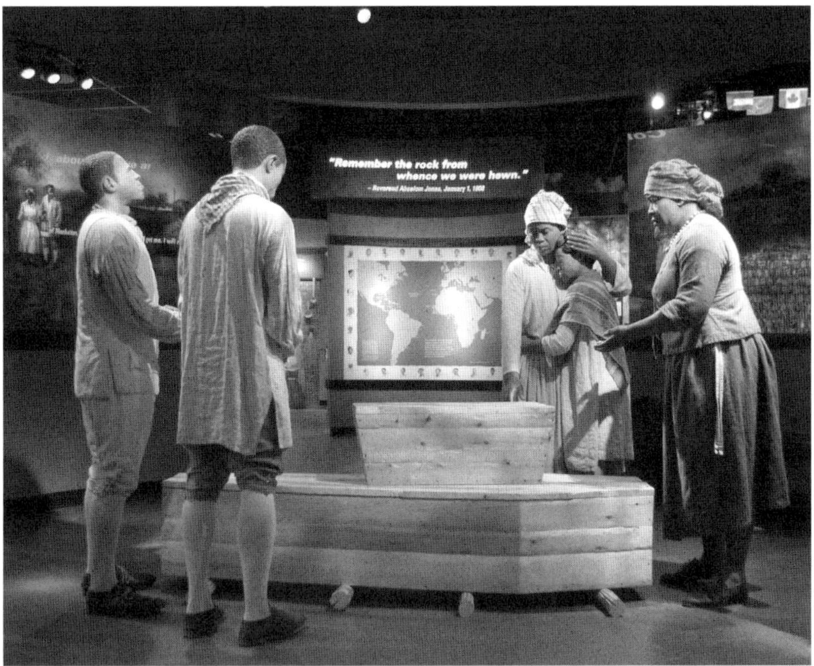

The burial scene at the African Burial Ground National Monument in lower Manhattan is brought to life by a subtle sound installation. Photo courtesy of Amaze Design, Inc.

based on meticulous historical research.[15] A more recent and modest example incorporating the use of sound comes from the African Burial Ground National Monument in lower Manhattan, where hundreds of people of African descent were buried in the Colonial era. The visitor encounters a burial scene—a small coffin on top of a larger one, with several life-size figures surrounding it—and hears an audio track of the mourners' words, cries, and songs.[16]

Sound can be subtle and still powerful. Robben Island Museum in Cape Town, South Africa, was a prison for political leaders during the apartheid era. As visitors step inside, the guide slams the metal doors shut, evoking a visceral sense of the terror and isolation prisoners like Nelson Mandela must have known. To increase the dramatic impact of the final section of *Choosing to Participate*, the story of Cambodian American Arn Chorn-Pond, we used flute music played by Arn himself. In formative evaluation, teenagers had a gratifyingly intense response to the music; one remarked that it transported her to another place.

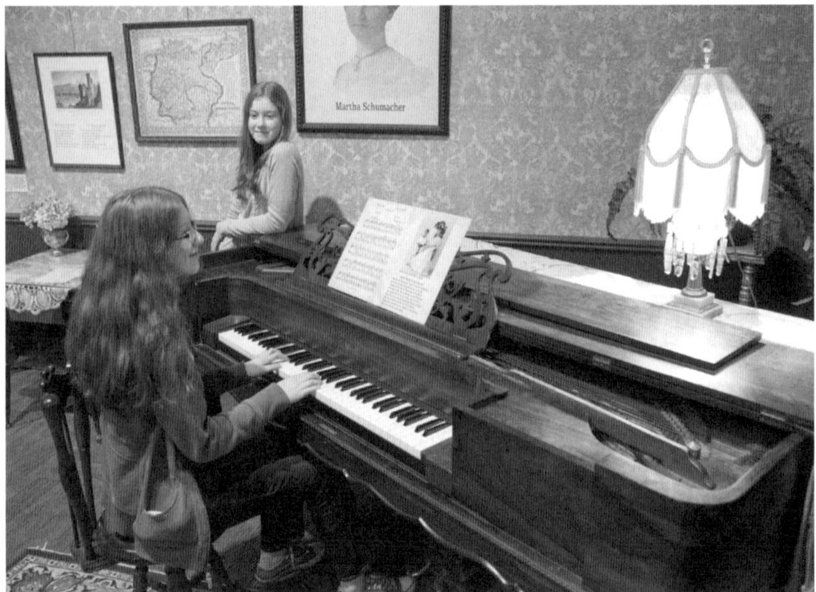

Open House: If These Walls Could Talk has many multi-sensory experiences for the visitor including a piano in the Schumacher's parlor; the approach of a visitor sets off a Schumann melody, a favorite of the eldest Schumacher daughter. Courtesy of Eric Mortenson, Minnesota History Center.

Children's and science museums employ the sense of smell most often, in my experience. But it is surprising that exhibition teams at other museums don't use it more often.[17] This story reminds us of the powerful association between smell and memory:

> My earliest recollection of doing anything in a museum was . . . [at the Brooklyn Children's Museum]. And we were making candles. And I remember that you got a piece of wood, and they tied some sort of—the wick, I guess—and they taught us some kind of song, and they had a table in the middle with hot wax. And here are the little kids, we're marching around with our wooden stick, and we are dipping—every time we got to where the vat was, you would dip your stick in and you would do some funny thing. And then of course as you walked around, the candle got fatter and fatter.
>
> I can remember it was bayberry scents. To this day when I smell bayberry I get like a crazy woman. I had this bayberry candle until I

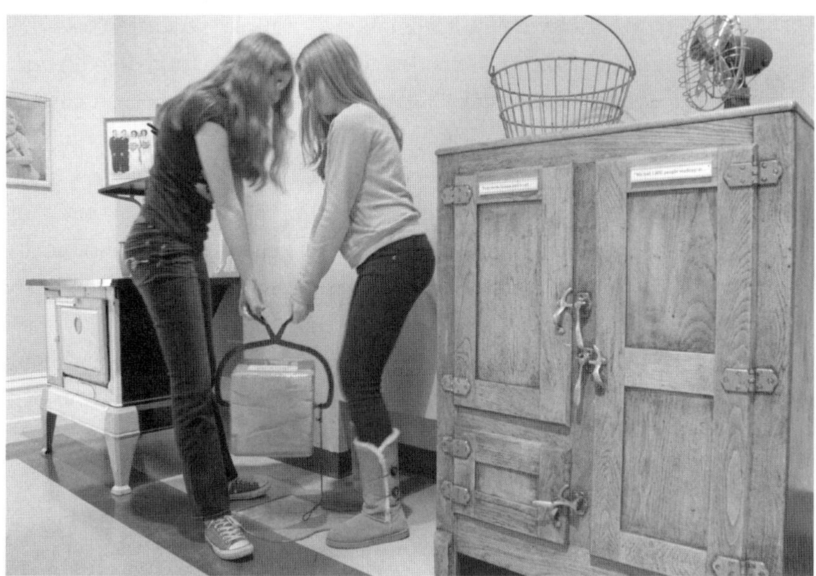

In the 1930s-era kitchen, visitors strain to pick up a block of ice.
Courtesy of Eric Mortenson, Minnesota History Center.

> was married. . . . And I was nineteen then. That's what it meant to me. I bought three bayberry candles three years ago so I could put them in my house and light them, so my house could smell of bayberry, because it was such a happy thing (M. Spock 1992, 19.25; 2000b, 22; Spock and Leichter 1999, 46).[18]

After the sense of sight, the sense of touch is probably most typically invoked in exhibitions. Here is a vivid example of how somatic or embodied imagination works in the *Open House* exhibition. In the 1930s-era Italian-American kitchen, complete with period icebox, visitors can lift a big block of ice. Two 21-year-old women responded in this way:

> *M1:* What's that?
>
> *M2:* A block of ice . . .
>
> *M1:* Give it a lift . . .
>
> *M2:* It's forty pounds.
>
> *M1:* Oh, my God! . . . (Ellenbogen et al. 2006a, 28)

Another, quite artful example is from the 120-year-old Eldridge Street Synagogue in Lower Manhattan, which reopened in 2007 as a sanctuary and museum after eleven years of meticulous restoration. It is a shimmering, color-drenched, majestic space with details that delight the eye in all directions. But according to Annie Polland, historian, museum educator, and author of *Landmark of the Spirit: The Eldridge Street Synagogue* (2009), the goal went beyond simply restoring this historic building. The restorers were storytellers; they wanted to capture the history of Eldridge Street and the vicissitudes of its immigrant population over time. So some places were left untouched. For instance, the worn pine floorboards kept the undulating grooves left by generations of worshippers shifting their feet in prayer. A visitor has only to step onto them to sense, in a powerful if inchoate way, those who were there before (Bedford 2012, 394).

While all exhibitions require visitors to move through them, the physicality of movement can be employed very intentionally. An exhibition at the Field Museum called *Inside Ancient Egypt* invites visitors to descend a spiral, dimly lit staircase into a tomb, a thrilling if disorienting experience that developer Janet Kamien felt helped turn visitors into time travelers (Bedford 2012, 398).

It may be that in employing one sense artfully, we make it more likely that visitors will believe their other senses are engaged as well. For instance, the boy who staggered out of the subway car in the *Teen Tokyo* exhibition (see chapter 4) hadn't actually experienced movement, but the sound effects coupled with other strategies created by the design team helped make him think he had. My own personal recollection of visiting the Eldridge Street Synagogue involves the creaking of old floorboards underfoot, but when I wrote to confirm this, I found out the boards, in fact, are silent.

One additional question concerns the cultural context for embodied experience. Pamela Erskine-Loftus, who works with museums in the Arabian Peninsula, writes about cross-cultural communication theory and museum practice. She argues that Western practice is "ocular-centric"; it privileges sight over other modes of perception (Erskine-Loftus 2013, 474). She mentions, for instance, how the use of "I see" in some languages connotes understanding as well as vision and how silent reading—of exhibit text, for example—is assumed to be the appropriate way of absorbing information. Arab cultures, on the other hand, are primarily audio-centric. Knowledge is shared socially and through oral traditions, and the transmission of texts is a "social activity creating relationships between the speaker and listener" (Erskine-Loftus 2013, 478). In considering how to make exhibitions more embodied experiences—as both neuroscience and past experience suggest we should—an examination of cultural differences could be fruitful as well.

Two final examples illustrate the ways in which exhibitions can employ *all* the senses together to inspire the visitor's imagination and generate understanding. *Dialogue in the Dark* began in Germany in 1988 and has traveled to 30 countries and 130 cities. Created to give sighted people an understanding of the challenges faced daily by the blind or visually impaired, its spaces simulate subway platforms, busy city streets, parks, and shops. But the visitors don't see them because the exhibition is utterly dark. Instead, they must rely on the sounds, smells, wind, temperatures, and textures around them, the long wands they clutch in their hands, and instructions from their guides, each of whom is partially or totally blind.[19] It is an extraordinary experience that, at least for the Bank Street graduate students with whom I visited it, created a profound empathy and respect for the visually impaired.

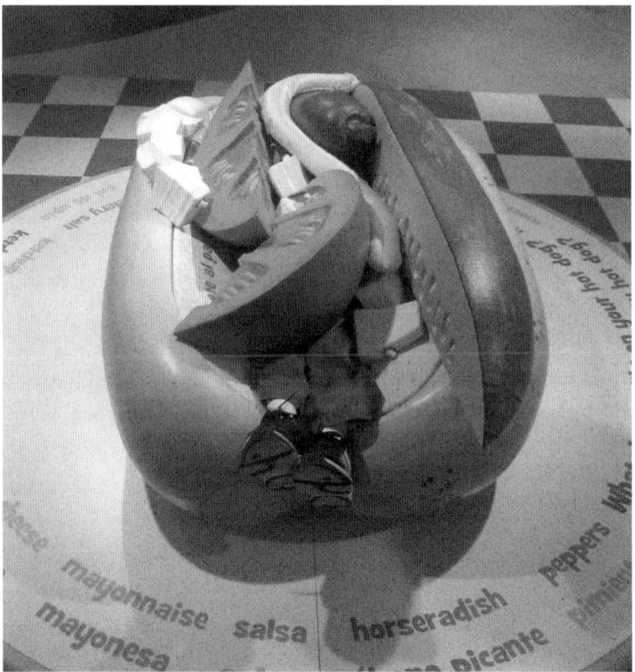

An exhibition that uses all the senses is *Sensing Chicago,* designed for families at the Chicago History Center. Here, eight-year-old Eli turns himself into a giant hot dog complete with condiments. Photo courtesy of Andrew Anway.

Design Mediates the Aesthetic Experience

Dewey says repeatedly that art doesn't *lead to* an experience; it *is* one (1934, 85). Scientists, he wrote, work "at one remove" from experience, but an aesthetic experience, as Annie Dillard's story about stopping to observe a sunset illustrates, is about being right there in the moment. The possibility for providing such an experience in exhibitions is heightened if the exhibition maker follows a familiar artistic imperative: Show me, don't tell me.

Geraldine Connolly's poem, "The Summer I Was Sixteen," uses concrete language to show rather than tell:

> The turquoise pool rose up to meet us,
> its slide a silver afterthought down which
> we plunged, screaming, into a mirage of bubbles.
> We did not exist beyond the gaze of a boy.
>
> Shaking water off our limbs, we lifted
> up from ladder rungs across the fern-cool
> lip of rim. Afternoon. Oiled and sated,
> we sunbathed, rose and paraded the concrete,
> danced to the low beat of "Duke of Earl."
> Past cherry colas, hot-dogs, Dreamsicles,
> we came to the counter where bees staggered
> into root beer cups and drowned. We gobbled
>
> cotton candy torches, sweet as furtive kisses,
> shared on benches beneath summer shadows.
> Cherry. Elm. Sycamore. We spread our chenille
> blankets across grass, pressed radios to our ears
>
> mouthing the old words, then loosened
> thin bikini straps and rubbed baby oil with iodine
> across sunburned shoulders, tossing a glance
> through the chain link at an improbable world.

Using all the tangible and resonant details of youth hanging around a summertime pool, Connolly enables us to enter into the moment. As Maxine Greene once remarked, poetry provides an answer that we cannot come to or provide didactically.

The aesthetic experience is not about teaching—the didactic telling—but closer to facilitating—the experiential showing or doing. This is a major reason stories work well; they provide for the listener's interior space, the imagination, to function and create an experience. It is difficult, perhaps impossible, for imaginative engagement to happen if someone else is telling you what to think.

Perhaps the exhibition team member most tasked with mediating the experience is the designer, the one who knows how to turn concepts into three-dimensional and visual experiences and underscore the unique detail and narrativity of each aspect.

Looking back at the Vietnam exhibition at the American Museum of Natural History, I wonder what it was about the display that enabled me to have the experience I had. The small shrine possessed both resonance and wonder; it provided an aesthetic experience, unique, complete, and expansive of meaning. If the box were simply left on the floor with a handwritten note, it would have interested (and puzzled) me, even made me think, but I am certain that it would neither have stopped me in my tracks, as it literally did, nor have left both a vivid image and strong emotions in its wake for weeks to come. Its artful arrangement of empty stone container, flowers, incense, and text etched on glass contributed to its power and was crafted with care by a designer.

As someone without a shred of design skill, I am always delighted by the ability of good designers to find strategies to express the concepts succinctly and artistically and help create the experience I was looking to provide. If they worked with language, they would be like the writers Bruner describes in *Actual Minds, Possible Worlds*: wordsmiths who know how to choose between boy, immature male, lad, or more metaphorically, colt, lamb, or fawn in describing a young male (Bruner 1986, 22), in order to find the vivid language that Annie Murphy Paul tells us fires up our mirror neurons.

The designer of *Choosing to Participate*, hearing over and over the phrase "step outside your circle of obligation" as shorthand for our main exhibition message, created a series of circles—some with people outside, others with people inside, others opened up. While simple, even obvious, and partially shaped by the needs of a traveling exhibition, this design choice mediated the experience in a totally nondidactic way.

This Philadelphia Story illustrates how design can facilitate a meaningful experience:

> I was part of the high school orchestra that played at the World's Fair in 1964. . . . And my brother was in the same orchestra. And we got some free time when we weren't playing, and we went to—it must have been the Italian [actually the Vatican] pavilion—and had an experience with the Pietà that had been brought over. And it was my first experience with a piece of art that was not just about culture and interesting. . . .
>
> And here was the Pietà, this beautiful sculpture . . . as I recall . . . there was a moving platform that we stood on in order to go in front of the Pietà. And then there was all this lighting that was changing, and there were curtains behind it. And I remember getting on the moving platform with my brother, and going by it, and being absolutely stunned and still. And when we got out of there we looked at each other and said, "Let's do it again." And we spent all afternoon going back in that line and going past that sculpture as often as we liked.
>
> And then the conversation that got going was about the lighting and how different—you know, how the faces looked, and how the marble was cut. And how could you do that with no modern tools? . . . How did they crate it and get it over from Italy? And wasn't it remarkable that it was there? And it was one of those experiences that I will never forget. And probably the first interactive experience I had in a museum, where a piece of art was done in a setting that changed it; that allowed it to show itself differently because of the lighting. Now I don't know if the lighting just changed because on the moving platform I saw the lights from different points, or if they really did change the lighting. I really don't know and I have never investigated what was the truth about my memory. I just know that I have this powerful memory of beautiful marble that looked as soft and—it was beholding. I mean it was there to be beheld in a very significant way. It was just beautiful (M. Spock 1992, 5.18).

But while design is the obvious first place to examine exhibition as art form, few designers see themselves as artists. Andy Merriell, the principal of an interpretive planning and design firm in New Mexico, says he is "in the business of packaging experience. I don't think like an artist but like a planner. Artists are self-motivated. I work for someone else. I am too much of a team player to be an artist" (Merriell 2005).

Designers, like exhibition developers, come to their work from various backgrounds and, until recently, without formal training in exhibition design.[20] Jim Volkert, another experienced designer, writes that there are three basic ways of thinking about exhibition design: as skill set, as art form, and as process and roles (Volkert 2006, 40–41). While the category of art form might best fit the current discussion, in his analysis, it is typically about matters of taste and style and apt to describe designers for whom neither the content nor the visitor is important. Volkert, Merriell, and all the designers I have mentioned are deeply committed to both.

Nevertheless, when pushed to describe how he worked on an inaugural exhibition, *All Roads Are Good: Native Voices on Life and Culture* at the National Museum of the American Indian's Heye Center in New York, Volkert revealed a process very reminiscent of the artistic. This exhibition included an acrylic case of moccasins arranged as if in a dance with space for one more pair, so the visitor could imagine joining in. Museum professionals often cite it as among their most memorable museum experiences.

Volkert explains how he and the curator, Gerald McMaster, worked together on its creation. They began with a metaphor: the gallery as a group of twenty-three elders talking together. McMaster uttered the phrase, "Walk a mile in my moccasins," and they began to see a mile-long band of moccasins circling the room. Volkert put some out on brown paper to play with, and McMaster said it all made him think that his ancestors were there, talking with him. This led to a circle, which in turn led to a dance. According to Volkert, these moments of creative synergy cannot happen without "no-fault play," and when a member of the staff—whether curator or designer—insists there is only one way of doing things, it kills the creativity and the possibility (Volkert 2005).

Unquestionably, exhibition design is an instrumental or applied art in service to content selected by someone else. And furthermore, designers usually work on teams without the solitary artist's freedom to play. Nonetheless, their process is part of the creation of an opportunity for an aesthetic experience—if that is their intention. Certainly the process Volkert describes for *All Roads Are Good* recalls Dewey's thoughts on the making and doing of art:

> In English we separate artistic and esthetic and the act of production and that of perception and enjoyment but they are integrated . . . . Man whittles, carves, and sings, dances, gestures, molds, draws and paints. The doing or making is artistic when the perceived result is of

> such a nature that its qualities as perceived have controlled the question of production. The act of producing that is directed by intent to produce something that is enjoyed in the immediate experience of perceiving has qualities that a spontaneous or uncontrolled activity does not have. The artist embodies in himself the attitude of the perceiver while he works. The esthetic experience—in its limited sense—is thus seen to be inherently connected with the experience of making (Dewey 1934, 47).[21]

Yet again, there is a continuum. At one end are the works of someone like Fred Wilson, a recognized artist who creates exhibitions explicitly as art; on the other is the lackluster and didactic exhibition whose design has been totally suffocated by content. In between are artistry and the potential for aesthetic experience.

Darwin at the American Museum of Natural History proved to be closer to an aesthetic experience than I anticipated. The design team worked hard to speak to visitors' emotions as well as their intellect, to make them understand and even care about Darwin's personal journey toward the publication of *On the Origin of Species* and then, having ignited our embodied selves, to help us appreciate the importance of his contribution to science. Fossils artfully displayed with a small magnifying glass, an elegant evocation of the Victorian era, also became a metaphor for Darwin's life of learning through close observation. The fossils were stunning; I overheard one visitor exclaim about a coiled snake skeleton, "How beautiful!" A narrative approach framed the entire exhibition and each of its sections, including the poignant story of Darwin's young daughter Annie's death—"Our Dear, Dear Child"—rendered especially moving by the collection of childhood treasures her bereaved mother put together. In a section called "Sandwalk," visitors viewed a continuous loop of a condensed-time video that had been taken every five feet along the "thinking path," the actual garden path that Darwin trod every day—an innovative example of trying to put visitors in someone else's shoes.

The last section of *Darwin* produced a sense of completion. The wall text—"Endless form most beautiful"—implies that the theory of evolution *can* support a spiritual view of the world—an issue raised throughout the show and exemplified by a display of living orchids. In other words, these choices turned this exhibition into *an* experience, one in which each stage sums up the values in what has preceded and evokes those that are yet to

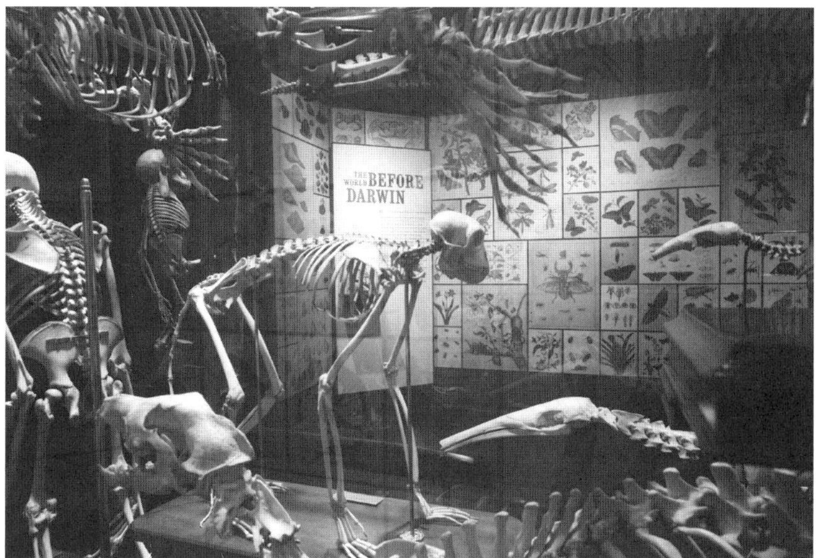

The artful design of this case of fossils reinforces their aesthetic qualities. Photo by Denis Finnin, ©American Museum of Natural History.

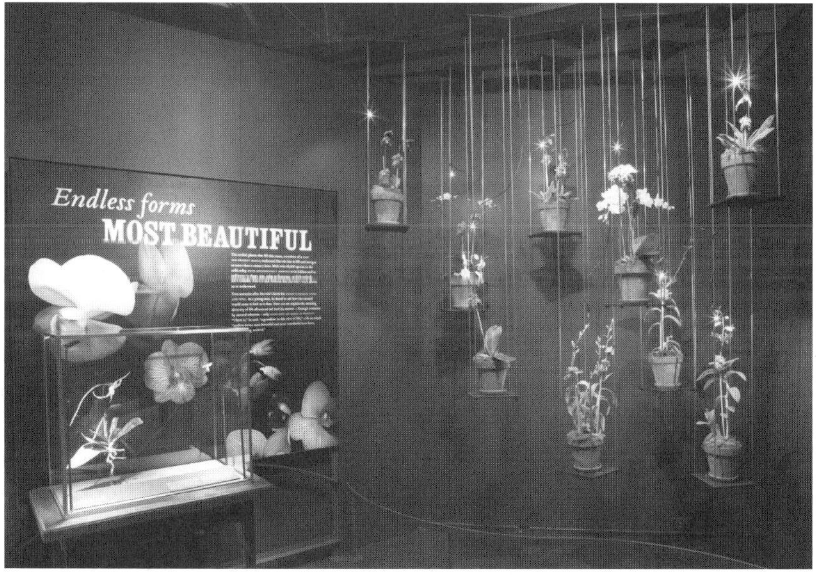

"Endless Forms Most Beautiful" captures the central narrative of *Darwin* at the American Museum of Natural History. Photo by Denis Finnin, ©American Museum of Natural History.

come. *Darwin* thus illustrates Dewey's ideas of completeness and continuity within itself, raised in chapter 5: "The connectedness must be such as brings the experience not merely to a close, but to a closure. The experience runs its course to fulfillment . . . Its close is a consummation and not a cessation" (1934, 42).

In recent years, the term *experience design* has emerged in the museum field, allegedly in response to the ubiquitous phrase *experience economy*. According to Donna Braden, Ellen Rosenthal, and Dan Spock (2005), experience design means using deliberate design strategies to create experience rather than transmit knowledge—in other words, using design to do what museum professionals have been talking about for many years.

At the Abraham Lincoln Presidential Library and Museum, the exhibit design plays to the visitors' emotions from the beginning, and uses their predictable responses to pull them through the narrative. Nearly every key episode in Lincoln's life is framed to take advantage of the potential of the concrete and specific to evoke the universal: the death of a parent, loss of a first sweetheart, rapture of true love, wrenching (though fictive) encounter with a family being sold into slavery, and so forth. But in the section narrating Lincoln's years in the White House, the designers—BRC Imagination Arts—pull out all the stops. Visitors encounter a life-size diorama of young Willie Lincoln sick in bed—his anxious parents having left a gala (sounds of music) to check on him (Abe, with toy in hand). Visitors then turn the corner and confront Willie's picture draped in black crepe. Finally, the exhibit leads to a disconsolate Mary Todd Lincoln, now in black, rocking slowly before a rain-splattered window, tears gathering in her sad eyes. It is hard not to be moved by this, although a deep suspicion of being manipulated arises as well.

Technology Creates the Feeling of Being There

Technology is an essential part of any designer's toolkit, in part because it makes possible things we once only dreamed of. Just as object theater enabled the *Teen Tokyo* design team to install Tetsuo's Room, a highly realistic domestic setting without the maintenance headaches of the existing three-dimensional Japanese House exhibition, so Mill City Museum in Minneapolis can take visitors on a journey into the history of the flour mill through a highly inventive computer-driven show installed in the factory's old elevator.

Likewise, a 25-foot-long interactive table, designed by Potion, a New York-based firm, in the Lower East Side Tenement Museum's new exhibit, *Shop Life*, allows the museum for the first time to tell multiple stories of a single space over the years. Visitors choose an object to place on the tabletop, triggering a series of images, oral histories, and text that become visible to tell the story of the shops that occupied the ground floor of 97 Orchard Street: a kosher butcher shop at the turn of the twentieth century, an auction house in the 1930s, a lingerie store in the 1970s. Several videos feature current stories of immigrants and commercial life.

Thanks to technology, public access to museum collections has been rendered both deep and respectful of people's desire to create their own meanings. It also allows the opportunity to find and comment on the many layers of meanings others have experienced.[22]

The various technologies now available to designers (when clients can afford them) can provide something called *presence*, a term often used in video games and virtual reality and "defined loosely as 'the feeling of being there'" (McMahan 2003, 69–70). In an old-fashioned medium like theater—or literature—the viewer has to be an active interpreter of the narrative. But technology can essentially do that work for you—that is, break down the so-called fourth wall more easily. The exhibitions I've mentioned contain numerous examples: the condensed-time video loop of Darwin's "thinking path," the subway car in *Teen Tokyo*, and the sound installations of the Pequot Museum or African Burial Ground.

How does technology contribute to working in the subjunctive mood? While it enables the telling of stories, the creation of presence, and the possibility for participation, dialogue, and shared meaning-making, it is only one of the strategies available, and it has to be in service, in my opinion, to the principles derived from story, imagination, and aesthetic experience. Some argue, for example, that in the digital age when information can be accessed randomly online rather than in a sequential or narrative mode, we may be moving into new patterns of thinking beyond the story form. (This intriguing idea has been explored extensively in literature and film—for example, Julio Cortazar's novel *Hopscotch* and the 2000 film *Memento.*) But designers of interactive media for exhibitions and elsewhere continue to work from a storyline. As Mike Jones, a technologist, author, and consultant, recently explained in an interview on designer Seb Chan's blog, *Fresh & New(er):*

> I think what we have to recognize is that technology has never actually changed what a story is. No story-telling technology is near so huge in impact as Radio was to a previously Theatrical and Literary culture. And yet a Radio Play conforms to all the same principles of character, tension, action, catharsis and transformation as a book, play or movie for that matter.
>
> The technology changed what mechanics you had at your disposal to tell that story but it didn't change what a story was or why people wanted them, what engaged and satisfied them (Jones 2012).

Nonetheless, it is clear that technology will continue to alter not only visitor expectations for the museum visit but also how exhibitions are designed and experienced. As we break down the fourth wall more and more, will the resultant higher level of "presence" generate a new medium, or simply a more effective version of the one we currently have? Will higher presence guarantee more of *an* experience with a greater expansion of meaning, or will it provide something engaging but utterly unmemorable, closer to recognition rather than perception, leaving us entertained but unmoved? From my perspective, technology that is employed in the service of story, imagination, and aesthetic experience can only heighten the rich potential of exhibitions to matter to visitors.

Theatricality Welcomes Visitors into the Narrative

As explained earlier, two basic elements make up narrative: the story itself—what happened—and then the narrative discourse, the way a particular medium, whether book, film, video game, or exhibition, tells it. Each medium has its own challenges and opportunities, but exhibition is the only one that can be "a fully embodied experience of objects and media in three-dimensional space, unfolding in a potentially free-flowing temporal sequence" (Macleod et al. 2012, xxi).[23] No other art form can claim this particular mix, with the possible exception of theater. And so it isn't surprising that several of the exhibitions I've mentioned were created by professionals with theatrical backgrounds or instincts: Jim Sims (*Field to Factory*), Brad Thiel (*Open House*), Janet Kamien (*Inside Ancient Egypt*), and Darcie Fohrman (*Daniel's Story*). Their work challenges us to think about the ways in which exhibition resembles theater and how such a perspective supports the subjunctive mood.

Theatrically-inclined designers create a threshold experience for visitors that makes them feel welcome and secure in their knowledge of what follows; this is the *liminal space*, an anthropologist's term for transitional rites or times. It is the space, real or metaphorical, between the ordinary and the extraordinary, the known and the unknown—that is, the imagined world of an exhibition. *Open House* creates this transitional moment with a friendly and reassuring invitation by an open door:

> **Open House: If These Walls Could Talk**
>
> What stories lie inside one ordinary house? To find out, we picked a real, existing house and dug into its past. Fifty families lived at 470/472 Hopkins Street on St. Paul's East Side across 118 years. Come explore their stories.

Inside Ancient Egypt does it somatically. One enters the exhibition by walking down into a (partially re-created) Egyptian tomb. Many exhibitions use media to create a feeling of presence, of being in a new reality—from soundtracks or simple projections on scrims to elaborate media presentations, such as *Freedom Rising*, which integrates media and live performance to orient visitors to Philadelphia's National Constitution Center.

One of the most effective and popular methods is theatrical programming. Museum theater is its own interdisciplinary field and supports an enormous range of practices. Examples include a permanent stage and residential theater company, such as City Stage at the Boston Children's Museum; floor staff trained in theatrical techniques, like those at Imagine It! The Children's Museum of Atlanta; intensive immersion through consistent first-person interpretation like that at Plimoth Plantation or Mount Vernon; scheduled programs or tours by actors, such as the Lower East Side Tenement Museum's Victoria Confino program; or, most typical of all, the addition of period costumes and props to provide a sense of place through third-person interpretive techniques at historic houses and sites. According to Dale Jones, a longtime practitioner and consultant on museum theater, the point is really to bring static space to life for visitors. He points to the longitudinal study by the Centre for Applied Theatre Research at the University of Manchester, which evaluated four different kinds of theatrical programs in Great Britain and underscores the value they add to the museum experience.[24]

But it is also possible to design the exhibition itself in a more theatrical way—for example, to cast the visitors intentionally as the actors. They are then pulled into the narrative, invited to interact with the artifacts and scenery and mingle with the other participants the exhibit team provides—characters made present through recorded voices, projected faces and scenes, soundscapes, and other media—and encouraged to enact the story themselves. These visitors are granted the right, the agency, to make things happen. *Open House* offers a variety of opportunities to affect the action—touching a silver dollar on a bureau in the 1950s bedroom to set off home movies on the mirror, or plopping down on a bed to initiate an oral history—along with hands-on activities such as the block of ice in the kitchen described earlier in this chapter. Throughout, the visitor-actor interprets the script that the museum provides, making meaning and also making history in the open-minded way the exhibition team intended. There is even a kind of Aristotelian unity to the story. We begin the visit to the house with an immigrant family in their front parlor and end with an immigrant family in their living room. One is German American, the other Vietnamese American. But perhaps this unity is only in the visitor's imagination?

Field to Factory drew heavily on theatricality. The first section, the South, is revealed behind a scrim; one glimpses figures bent over their work outside half-ruined wooden buildings. Curator Spencer Crew wanted visitors to understand that these wooden shacks were home, that heading north meant deep loss. The designer's job was to create this inchoate understanding in the visitor. Once you leave "home," you must enter the railroad station—choosing the door for White or Colored—for the train north to the factories. Visitors re-create the journey made by millions of people, but they add their own individual sensibilities.

The United States Holocaust Memorial Museum took a different approach in its permanent exhibition: visitors are bystanders to the story, witnesses to what happened and what did not. After observing a photo collage showing people being deported to the concentration camps, you walk through a railroad car and are faced with images of Nazi officers splitting families apart, selecting some for work and others to be killed. The perspective of witnessing is underscored in the museum's main atrium with a quote from the bible that says "you are my witnesses" (Isaiah 43:10).

Each of these iconic exhibitions—all historical narratives—illustrates how the confines of a strict chronology can be opened up. Because the exhibitions involve personal choice, somatic experiences, narrativity rather than didacticism in the text, powerfully evocative and often metaphorical objects—like the milk can remembered above to anchor the plot—and other invitations to individual interpretation and participation, they transcend the more traditional forced march of many historical exhibitions. Conventional wisdom would hold that visitors must be free to go how and where they choose, but these exhibitions depend on pursuing a particular path. But they do that through a deft combination of fact and feelings. Unlike the intensely technology-driven storytelling of the Lincoln Museum, these narratives honor the meaning of *an* experience, of perception over recognition, and of the need for imagination to be given enough breathing space.[25]

Authenticity Is the Yardstick for Meaningful Experiences

In *Art as Experience,* Dewey contrasts artistic to scientific truth:

> In an intellectual experience [i.e., scientific inquiry], the conclusion has value on its own account. It can be extracted as a formula or as a "truth," and can be used in its independent entirety as factor and guide in other inquiries. In a work of art there is no such single self-sufficient deposit. The end, the terminus, is significant not by itself but as the integration of the parts. It has no other existence. A drama or novel is not the final sentence, even if the characters are disposed of as living happily ever after (Dewey 1934, 55).

Bruner's analysis of the paradigmatic versus the narrative mode centers on a similar distinction. As mentioned earlier, he notes that both modes can be used to convince someone of something, "yet what they convince *of* is fundamentally different: arguments convince one of their truth, stories of their lifelikeness" (Bruner 1986, 11; italics added).

If one were to reframe exhibitions as aesthetic rather than purely educational experiences, how should we think about "truth"? Once the exhibition field began to embrace narrative—or, in educational language, constructivism—over the transmission of knowledge, it had to acknowledge, if not privilege, the creation of personal meaning over the uncovering of truth. If visitors are looking for meaning and measuring their encounters by the yardstick of personal authenticity ("it seems right to me"), then they are approaching exhibitions in the way Northrop Frye talks about theater:

> The poet's job is not to tell you what happened, but what happens: not what did take place, but the kind of thing that always takes place. He gives you the typical, recurring, or what Aristotle calls universal event. You wouldn't go to *Macbeth* to learn about the history of Scotland—you go to it to learn what a man feels like after he's gained a kingdom and lost his soul (Frye 1964, 64).

How are we to reconcile this with a professional commitment to scholarship as well as the public's professed faith in museums as truth tellers? This question came up frequently in the development of *Choosing to Participate*, including the design of a new component. This section tells the story of Arn Chorn-Pond, a childhood survivor of the Cambodian killing fields who eventually escaped to a refugee camp and was adopted by an American aid worker named Peter Pond. The goal is to help young visitors understand that everyone has a story—for example, the foreign kid sitting next to you in math class—and that telling and listening can also be acts of participation.

In developing the section, the design team wrestled with the question of whose version of the story is the true one. How do we reconcile Arn's unhappy version of his early tumultuous days at a rural American high school with what we later learned was the school's sympathetic and intensive efforts to make him feel at home? The former perspective is what gives the story resonance with young visitors; the latter is part of the actual record. To what extent have the different perspectives changed with time and with the very human desire to put things in a positive light? The answer was to respect the multiple versions of the truth and let the visitors, as they inevitably will, make up their own minds, while at the same time permitting Arn's story—the dramatic, aesthetic experience, so to speak—to set the stage. Another approach was employed in the creation of *Daniel's Story* at the Holocaust Museum, as the staff created a fictional Daniel whose life details were based on exhaustive research to mirror typical experiences.

The team designing *Open House* faced some similar challenges. The goal was to "encourage visitors to explore the interconnections between 'story,' 'memory,' and 'history'" (Minnesota Historical Society 2003). In this effort, the team included both typical and atypical aspects of the various time periods depicted in the house. The historical research was prodigious, often contributing ephemeral details that enhanced an unfolding narrative of everyday life over time.

Framing exhibitions as aesthetic experience enables one to work in a zone between imagination and rigorous concern for the historical record. For example, addressing its declining visitation, which reflects a nationwide problem, a living history museum decided to evaluate its interpretive strategies. A couple of staff members were eager to bring more unique and dramatically rich details to their well-established tableau of generic nineteenth-century village life. But others feared that if, for instance, the new narrative included the one person they had found in the historical record who believed in hanging garlic wreaths to ward off vampires, then visitors would think all nineteenth-century Americans shared such superstitions. But the model of exhibition as aesthetic experience shows us that specific, concrete detail is precisely what generates meaning making. It doesn't yield some kind of abstract principle or textbook interpretation ("American Rural Religious Beliefs: The Role of Vampires in the 19th Century"), but rather a series of imaginative reflections: "Gosh, I wonder how many people did this? I wonder why he believed in vampires? Did anyone else? Or even, perhaps, I wonder if garlic really works?"

Writers assume their readers are likely to either "under-read" or "over-read" a narrative (Abbott 2002, 79–83). But in the museum field, despite its tentative embrace of constructivism, we often insist that as long as different learning styles are acknowledged, the same content can be taught to all our visitors. In my opinion, we are more wedded to the "truth," the social scientist's goal—the paradigmatic—than to the "authentic"—the yardstick for storytellers and artists. But given that exhibitions exist in the imagined, constructed world that is created and interpreted by exhibition developer/designer and visitor, might not the goal of the "authentic"—of truth as "the uncovering of meaning"—be the more appropriate choice? I would suggest that the exhibitions that people—including myself—find most memorable are those that strike the human chord, that resonate with what we believe and feel to be true.

In creating an exhibition about a period in time, a culture, or the theory of evolution, the "truth"—the record—absolutely must be respected if museums are to remain trusted guardians of cultural heritage. But if we are no longer in the business of transmitting knowledge, then we need a different language for describing and understanding what we do. And that can be found in the arts. In other words, Freeman Tilden, the architect of historic interpretation, had it right when he described a colleague in this way:

> He thoroughly enjoyed his stay upon this planet, which he found so full of a number of things . . . and he enjoyed pointing out these things in a new light. . . . He never forgot that the feeling of an exhibit and the need for it to tell a story were quite as important as its factual truthfulness (quoted in Ott 2001).

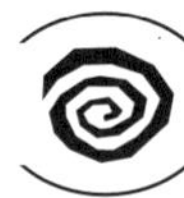

Conclusion

Like the geese Maxine Greene said cause the ducks to stand on tiptoe, certain exhibitions inspire us to work in the subjunctive mood of story, imagination, and aesthetic experience. For me, another exhibition that embraces these elements particularly well is *Noah's Ark* at the Skirball Cultural Center in Los Angeles. The audience is families and children—not surprising, since my background in children's museums has convinced me we grant ourselves more freedom in working with that group than in more adult and discipline-based settings.

The space in *Noah's Ark* is framed by the story of the flood, a universal master plot, which front-end evaluation showed had cross-cultural resonance and familiarity for the audience. This story provides a strong but flexible framework on which to hang a multitude of activities, ideas, and values. We are pulled into the narrative through a variety of multisensory experiences, such as highly transparent rain- and wind-making interactives and simple, often poetic "gobo text" projected on the polished floors ("Wind whispers," "Coyotes call").

The huge wooden ark is itself a work of art, as are many of the fanciful animals made of recycled materials designed by Chris Green, a sculptor and puppeteer. Some are folk art from various cultures, others stuffed toys for cuddling or carrying around. The exhibit offers reading nooks, a climbing sculpture, a light projection to stand in and wonder about—multiple means of engaging children's imaginations and learning modalities. And as the story ends and we emerge from the ark, the exhibit asks, "How can we build a better world?" and invites us to post our thoughts at a computer kiosk. A white dove made of wooden spindles flies overhead, the appropriate olive branch in it mouth.

Leslie Bedford, "Conclusion" in *The Art of Museum Exhibitions: How Story and Imagination Create Aesthetic Experiences*. pp. 129–133.

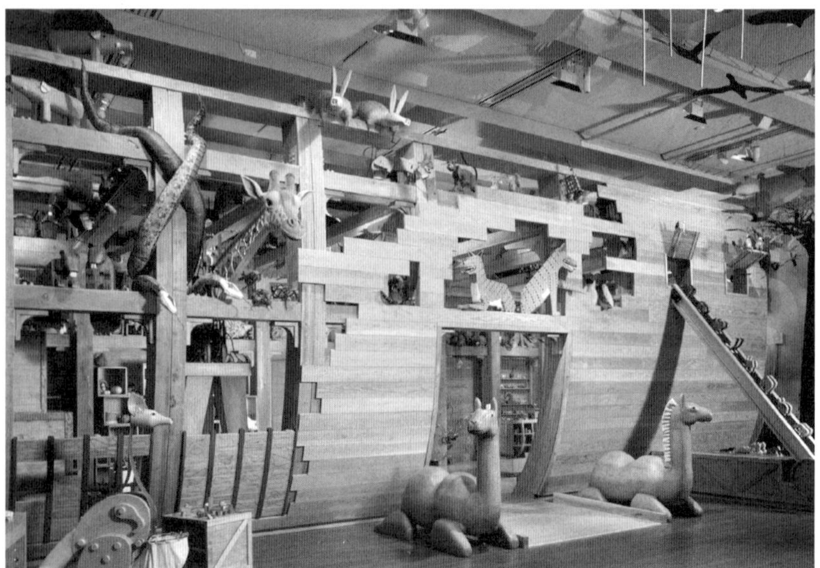

Noah's Ark combines story, imagination, and aesthetic experience to delight its family audience. Photo by Grant Mudford. Courtesy of Skirball Cultural Center.

Noah's Ark was expensive to make. Few institutions have such resources, but, as I hope I have demonstrated, such exhibitions depend on much more than money to succeed. They require not only an excellent team and way of working but also the habits of mind I have been proposing for exhibition development.

The inquiry I began with my doctoral studies in 2001 focused on what exhibitions are for, what I love about them, and why so many disappoint me. The best way I found to approach those questions was to return to my friend's compliment about *Teen Tokyo*—the remark with which I began this book: that exhibitions are a form of art and aesthetic experience, and their makers work as artists. Despite my years of teaching, I wasn't satisfied by the field's insistence on exhibition as educational medium. Some of that was definitional; education, or learning, was becoming such a broad term that it was losing meaning for me. But much of it reflected my growing fascination with the idea of imagining as the fundamental mental, emotional, and physical process I was beginning to explore through the various theories I've labeled my tent poles. As I hope I have made clear, imagination and aesthetic experience are deeply connected to learning, and learning is central to the museum experience.

Aesthetic experience and imagination are old ideas in the museum field, and they continue to inform professional practice, especially in art institutions. But they are rarely invoked in the visitor-centered way I am using these terms. Among more progressive practitioners in all kinds of institutions, they have been supplanted by concern for participation, accessibility, diversity, civic engagement, and other aspects of public value. These goals are worthy and also deeply important to me. But as a practitioner I wasn't convinced they helped us figure out *how* to make the experience of an exhibition meaningful. We have learned over the years to respect individual responses: everyone is different, and thus there is no one answer. That's why the Philadelphia Stories are powerful; they reveal the individual voices of visitors. I wanted to find some way of honoring our differences as well as the unique nature of our most important medium. I hoped that I might also uncover something that would ultimately support the importance of museums as public partners in promoting social democracy and well-being. I thought empathy for others was an important and appropriate goal, but I was pretty sure that using exhibitions to tell people what to do with their lives didn't work. As *New York Times* critic Charles Isherwood wrote, "Good art does not, of course, deliver messages like moral telegrams."[1]

But, as I was trained years ago to ask before and during the exhibition process: So what? What difference does it make if exhibitions use story, imagination, and aesthetic experience? Does the subjunctive mood make any real contribution to the people who visit museums? I don't have an answer to those questions, though I am hoping readers will contribute their own ideas. But there are some thoughts worth sharing.

Recently I came across an article by Mark O'Neill, whose work at Kelvingrove and other Glasgow museums—and his fierce commitment to accessibility of all kinds—has inspired many in the field. This short piece, "Cultural Attendance and Public Mental Health—From Research To Practice," summarizes recent research around the world into the public health benefits of cultural attendance. As he notes, many institutions have learned how intensive engagement with cultural activities—art workshops, for example—can benefit people who have been left out of mainstream cultural activities. But other research now suggests that even occasional involvement in such activities (movies, art exhibits, live popular music, plays, and so on) makes a difference in longevity and well-being, regardless of income, educational level, age, gender, or level of physical activity. And according to an Israeli study, the impact holds true whether or not the activity involves being with others or alone, such as solitary reading. The tentative conclusion—and the article avoids generalizing from what is only preliminary research—reminds us that a "key characteristic of cultural experiences is that they enrich the sense of life being meaningful" (O'Neill 2010, 25). On the assumption that "cultural attendance makes an essential contribution to the quality of life, and should form an integral part of any public health policy" (O'Neill 2010, 26), the city of Glasgow is implementing policies to enable its cultural institutions to reach out to and welcome the broadest possible constituency, in particular, first-time users.

What is it that cultural activities, including reading, give us that is so important to our sense of well-being—or, as Mihaly Csikszentmihalyi put it, our basic happiness?

A recent study published in the journal *Science* shows that people who had just read literary fiction performed better on tests measuring empathy, social perception, and emotional intelligence than those who had read popular fiction or serious nonfiction. These are the skills associated with theory of mind, mentioned in chapter 3. These skills begin to develop in early childhood and are essential to understanding our relationships with other people. The researchers suggest that literary fiction often leaves more to the imagination, encouraging readers to make inferences about characters and be sensitive to emotional nuance and complexity. They postulate that theory of mind "may be influenced by engagement with works of art."[2]

This perspective recalls Maxine Greene's view that engagement with a work of art can "move persons to think about alternative ways of being alive, possible ways of inhabiting the world" (1985, 32). And it is very close to empathy, which is the ability to understand and share the feelings of another. It also relates to Kieran Egan's definition of imagination as "the ability to think of the possible, not just the actual" (chapter 4). In imagining, we are moving beyond our immediate reality to become open to new ways of thinking and doing. Change must be imagined before it can be implemented, and thus, as Greene says, "to learn . . . is to choose against things as they are" (1988, 45).

Another approach to the question of "So what?" resides in thinking about what museums offer us: evidence of our human history and those narratives that give meaning to our lives. Mark O'Neill explores the connections between museums and the most fundamental narrative of all—human mortality—in

"Museums and Mortality," a complex analysis of two scholarly approaches to understanding death and dying.[3] Central to the discussion is his point that "the primary cultural task [for museums is] . . . creating meaning in the face of mortality" (O'Neill 2012, 69).

A companion narrative to mortality is time. Inspired by Adam Gopnik's 2007 piece, "The Mindful Museum," I wrote that museums enable us to contemplate the meaning of time: "What could be more important to us than our relationship to time? Life, love, death, family—time is definitely one of those universal Big Ideas" (Bedford 2012, 393). I mentioned the work of psychologist Daniel Kahneman who says we have two selves: "the 'experiencing self,' who is living life as it goes on in the moment, and the 'remembering self,' who is recapturing and creating the story of his past." Museums provide "an opportunity for our two selves—experiencing and remembering—to collaboratively empower objects, language, settings, and artistry to spark the endlessly generative process of making meaning, making story, and understanding time" (Bedford 2012, 399).

We are embodied storytellers, endowed with imagination and capable of making meaning. And as many of the colleagues I have mentioned in this book have pointed out, the making of meaning is not only what we do every day, but what gives value to human existence. We are also learners and social beings who enjoy play and seek pleasure. Museums can and do respond to all these needs—and many others—in various ways with varying degrees of intentionality and success. Just as each visitor is different and comes to us with his or her personal agenda, no exhibition can respond to everything we ask of it. And certainly not every exhibition should be designed as an aesthetic experience. I have argued for a particular continuum, the one that I—with all the attributes that define me as an individual—personally found worth examining: one that begins with the fundamental search for story, bridges to the possibility of imagining, and moves into aesthetic experience. I think these elements of the subjunctive mood—in the hands of people who both acknowledge and also have the skills to employ them—are more likely to make a difference in our ongoing search for meaning and happiness.

Notes

Introduction

1. Of the seventy-five Spock transcripts, several have been published, some in more than one form, such as an individual journal article, as part of a video (and accompanying teacher's guide) called *Philadelphia Stories* (2000), or a chapter in a book about children's museums. Many remain unpublished.

1. For a detailed description of the Japan area, see Leslie Bedford and Leslie Swartz, "Cultural Learning: Two Models," in *Boston Stories* (M. Spock 2013, 192). This collection of case studies by museum staff members from the 1960s, 1970s, and 1980s candidly examines the programming, exhibitions, management structure, and fundamental values of this "laboratory for informal learning" while providing an excellent and beautifully illustrated history of the museum.

2. Object theater—pioneered by Taizo Miyake at Science North in Sudbury, Ontario, in the1980s—uses computer-based technologies to provide a theatrical experience much like a sound-and-light show. The Minnesota History Center created *My Home, Minnesota* in the 1990s, and the Boston Children's Museum developed an object theater—the re-creation of a Tokyo family's space called *Tetsuo's Room*—for the *Teen Tokyo* exhibition in 1992. Since then, the approach has become considerably more sophisticated, as in the library setting at the Abraham Lincoln Presidential Library and Museum in Springfield, Illinois (see chapter 6).

3. Having congratulated myself on "discovering" this felicitous turn of phrase, which I had earlier used in an article for *Curator* and assumed came to mind because I was studying Spanish at the time, I was chagrined to find it came from play theorist Brian Sutton-Smith (1988, 7) and had been used by Jerome Bruner and probably any number of others as yet undiscovered.

4. While one can safely say that most museum professionals concur in the educational purpose of exhibitions, it is worth noting that the field is hardly homogeneous. Still, there may be more common ground than previously thought.

Chapter 1

1. Of the seventy-five Spock transcripts, several have been published, some in more than one form, such as an individual journal article, as part of a video (and accompanying teacher's guide) called *Philadelphia Stories* (M. Spock 2000b), or a chapter in a book about children's museums. Many remain unpublished. The stories were solicited by a flyer sent out prior to two museum conferences. It read as follows:

   Tell Us Your Stories

   We are gathering interesting stories from our colleagues of significant, memorable, pivotal museum learning experiences for two research programs on learning in museums. These interviews will guide our research and be excerpted in useful publications and videotapes for the profession. Stop by for an interview or just pick up some materials about the project. Look for us and the Bright Lights! We will be stationed at various places throughout the conference to collect your fascinating observations about learning in museums (Spock and Leichter 1999, 42).

2. Wittlin went on to point out the differences between theory and reality: "In practice, the traditions of the former private collections were carried out in the public museums, notwithstanding the contrariety of purpose and circumstances" (quoted in Hein 2006, 2).

3. Worth noting is that in the years before the founding of major research universities, museums and museum curators were knowledge producers, as universities are today. Conn writes that the shift from knowledge production to dissemination coincides with the beginning of the museum shift toward teaching schoolchildren.

4. Hein notes, among other informational gems about the history of museum education, that for a period, museum educators eschewed the term education. It "had acquired such negative connotations for museum educators—implying obligatory, formal, fact-laden information transfer—that many in the museum world preferred to use the term interpretation (quoting Laurence Vail Coleman in Hein 2006, 1).

5. Gardner, *Frames of Mind: The Theory of Multiple Intelligences* (1983; 3rd ed. New York: Basic Books, 2011).

6. "Flow" is a concept enshrined in the museum field. It refers to the state of total involvement in an activity for its own sake. Exhibition developers are eager to create strategies that will spark this kind of intrinsic rather than extrinsic motivation for learning—something especially important when there is no teacher or facilitator on hand —but acknowledge how difficult it is to achieve.

7. The explosion of work in the field of museum education and interpretation is extraordinary. Readers are directed to Kris Wetterlund and Scott Sayre's listserv, museum-ed.org, as well as to the *Journal of Museum Education*, among other valuable sources.
8. After an early career at the Chicago Botanic Garden and the Field Museum of Natural History, Roberts spent ten years as director of the Garfield and Lincoln Park Conservatories for the Chicago Park District, where she developed innovative programs and community partnerships. She is now a teacher and consultant.
9. There is considerable research into why people visit museums and want to learn once they get there. In John Falk and Lynn Dierking's book *The Museum Experience Revisited* (2013), the authors summarize and update their research into motivation and identity; this book is discussed later in this chapter. See also Rounds 2004 and D. Spock 2006.The firm REACH Advisors has also published extensively on this issue.
10. For a curatorial perspective, see Nancy Villa Bryck, "Reports of Our Death Have Been Greatly Exaggerated: Reconsidering the Curator," *Museum News* 80, no. 2 (March/April 2001), 14.
11. In his introduction to *Art as Experience*, Abraham Kaplan interprets the concept of the active mind, a cornerstone of Dewey's philosophy of education, as emanating from late-nineteenth-century science, especially Darwinian thought and the centrality of "energy" (Kaplan 1981, xvii).
12. What is the difference between education and learning, and why has the former term lost favor in the literature? A website called differencebetween.com has a useful answer: Learning is knowledge gained through experience, and education is knowledge gained through teaching (http://www.differencebetween.net/miscellaneous/difference-between-education-and-learning, accessed December 17, 2013). This distinction is consistent with the field's embrace of an experiential model of education. In any case, in most of the literature, education refers to institutional structure and professional roles—educators in the education department—and learning to the process in which they and the visitor are collaboratively engaged. But there are those who worry that in abandoning the familiar term education, we have compromised our ability to influence governmental policies and funding.
13. Since then, other roles have proliferated: evaluators, graphic designers, media specialists, text writers, and representatives from marketing and public relations also often sit at the table. For a thorough introduction to the exhibition process, see McLean 1993 and McKenna-Cress and Kamien 2013. For a summary of major trends in the history of exhibitions, see McLean 1999.

14. The first visitor study was published in 1884 by the Liverpool Museum (Henry Hugh Higgins, "Museums of Natural History: Part I, Museum Visitors," *Transactions of the Literary and Philosophical Society of Liverpool,* 185–88), and the first funding for visitor studies came in the 1920s from the Carnegie Corporation for research on museum fatigue (Edward S. Robinson, *The Behavior of the Museum Visitor* [Washington, DC: American Association of Museums, 1928]). After that, the field languished until the 1960s. The Visitor Studies Association, a professional organization founded in 1988, is dedicated "to understanding and enhancing learning experiences in informal settings through research, evaluation, and dialogue." VSA publishes a biennial journal called *Visitor Studies*. I am indebted to George Hein for clarifying the history of this important aspect of museum work.
15. In keeping with Michael Spock's practice in some of his publications and respectful of the prominence of several of these voices in the field, I have not identified the museum professionals who contributed their stories.
16. "Mission Statement," *Facing History and Ourselves*, www.facinghistory.org/aboutus/missionstatement (accessed October 23, 2013).
17. For images, teacher resources, and exhibition guides, see the *Choosing to Participate* website, www.choosingtoparticipate.org, created by Facing History and Ourselves.
18. The team consisted of designer Fred Ellman (formerly with Roundtable Design), the multimedia design firm Russell Brosnahan Haffner Multimedia, Inc. (RBH), Guest Exhibition Production, and the author.
19. Since 1999, *Choosing to Participate* has been presented in both traditional venues, such as the New-York and Chicago Historical Societies, and unconventional ones, such as the main public libraries in Boston and Los Angeles. After a redesign in 2007 to include the inspiring and more contemporary story of Cambodian-American Arn Chorn-Pond in a section called "Everyone Has a Story," the exhibition reopened in Boston in January 2008. In 2011 it began its second tour to American cities with Facing History offices. The exhibition was cited in 2001 by *Time Out New York* as one of the five "best things" to have happened in New York City that year.
20. For two compelling manifestos on the value of museum education to the field, see Cutler 2012 and Garcia 2012.
21. There are very few places in the country where one can learn to become an exhibition developer. One is the University of the Arts in Philadelphia, which currently is developing a stronger track in program/exhibition development. The Fashion Institute of Technology, while knowledgeable, is mostly focused on design and designers. Bank Street College offers courses on exhibitions in both of its masters in museum education programs, as do many other museum education and museum studies programs across the country. But the best route

remains on-the-job training. As a result, in my opinion, one is apt to find the best exhibitions at institutions that continue to support their own in-house exhibition departments rather than using an outside design firm. It is not surprising that *Open House* at the Minnesota History Center is as good as it is. Both the head of the department and the several designers who worked on it had years of experience in developing visitor-centered, carefully researched and evaluated projects. Unfortunately, this combination of in-house expertise and experience has become a luxury today. It is, in any case, part of the discussion of the impact of institutional context.

Chapter 2

1. Nina Simon responded to museum critics' charges that art museums are losing their capacity for wonder and aesthetic contemplation in the face of new participatory technologies by asserting that these writers were out of touch with the needs of younger, more diverse audiences. Her post prompted considerable, generally favorable, discussion. Simon, "Open Letter to Arianna Huffington, Edward Rothstein, and Many Other Museum Critics," Museum 2.0, January 5, 2011, museumtwo.blogspot.com/2011/01/open-letter-to-arianna-huffington.html (accessed October 23, 2013).
2. NAGPRA requires federal agencies and institutions that receive federal funding to return Native American "cultural items" to lineal descendants and culturally affiliated Indian tribes and Native Hawaiian organizations. http://en.wikipedia.org/wiki/Native_American_Graves_Protection_and_Repatriation_Act (accessed October 23, 2013).
3. *Stewards of the Sacred* (ed. Lawrence E. Sullivan and Alison Edwards [Washington, DC: American Association of Museums, 2004]) is a recent attempt to grapple with the secular and the sacred in museums. Elaine Heumann Gurian's chapter, "Singing and Dancing at Night" (89–96) is especially relevant to this discussion.
4. Lois H. Silverman is a scholar, writer, and consultant to museums. Her dissertation is entitled *Of Us and Other "Things": The Content and Function of Talk by Adult Visitor Pairs in an Art and a History Museum* (Indiana University, 1991).
5. Nina Simon, a former exhibit designer and museum consultant, is now executive director of the Santa Cruz Museum of Art and History in Santa Cruz, California. She writes the blog Museum 2.0: http://museumtwo.blogspot.com (accessed October 23, 2013).
6. Nina Simon, "The Event-Driven Museum, One Year Later," Museum 2.0, June 27, 2012, http://museumtwo.blogspot.com/2012/06/event-driven-museum-one-year-later.html (accessed October 23, 2013).

7. For more about *Unsilent Night,* see www.unsilentnight.com (accessed October 23, 2013). *Sleep No More* has received considerable interest from members of the museum community, who speculate on how exhibitions can be made more like interactive theater; see http://en.wikipedia.org/wiki/Sleep_No_More_%282011_play%29 (accessed October 23, 2013). The various projects of Flux Foundation, which can be viewed at http://fluxfoundation.org/category/portfolio/ (accessed October 23, 2013), include Colony, an interactive, collaborative project at the 2012 American Alliance of Museums' annual meeting in Minneapolis.

8. See Elaine Heumann Gurian, "Wanting to Be the Third on the Block," http://www.egurian.com/omnium-gatherum/museum-issues/leadership/directors-issues/wanting-to-be-the-third-on-your-block (accessed October 23, 2013).

9. An important addendum to the theme of participation comes from recent writings on the concept of public value, especially as articulated by Harvard professor Mark Moore in *Creating Public Value: Strategic Management in Government* (1995). Carol Scott, Mary Ellen Munley, and others have applied Moore's analysis of the strategic relationship between "the authorizing environment"—typically the political arena—"operational capacity," and "public value" to museums (see *Journal of Museum Education* 2010 for different perspectives). Scott's edited volume, *Museums and Public Value: Creating Sustainable Futures* (2013) offers the creation of a new gallery, *London, Sugar and Slavery*, at the Museum of London Docklands as an example of implementing public value precepts in exhibition development. Rather than being the passive recipients of work done on their behalf (the traditional model) or the more involved but still unempowered "informants" (for instance, by serving on visitor panels or community consultants), the public's role is theoretically closer to the actual "authorizing environment" (Spence et al. 2013, 99–109).

    As Lynn Dierking points out in "Being of Value: Intentionally Fostering and Documenting Public Value" (*Journal of Museum Education* 2010, 9–19), public value is anything but a new idea in the field—from John Cotton Dana and John Dewey to Stephen Weil and contemporary discussions of civic engagement, including community curation and co-curation of exhibitions. But Moore's theory supplies new energy to the enterprise in light of the twenty-first century's broader focus on participation.

10. Tom Hennes, conversation with the author. Jay Rounds has been a curator and museum director and served as E. Desmond Lee Professor of Museum Studies at the University of Missouri—St. Louis.

11. Stephen Greenblatt is a literary critic, John Cogan Professor of the Humanities at Harvard University, and winner of the 2012 Pulitzer Prize for general nonfiction for *The Swerve: How the World Became Modern*.

12. Kiersten Latham is an assistant professor in the School of Library and Information Science at Kent State University. With Elizabeth Wood, she is the author of *The Objects of Experience: Transforming Visitor-Object Encounters in Museums* (Walnut Creek, Calif.: Left Coast Press, 2013).
13. Latham writes that *numen* originally meant "a religious emotion or experience that can be awakened in the presence of something holy" (2007, 248) but has been adopted and expanded to include nonreligious objects and experiences in particular, like those in Greenblatt's category of resonance, involving "transcendental experience[s] that people can have in contact with a historic site or objects in an exhibit" (248).
14. This discussion is, admittedly, deeply U.S.-centric. Our colleagues around the globe are wrestling with many of the same ideas.
15. One could argue that, certainly among many practitioners, the museum's educational agenda was firmly established. But receiving substantial support from the National Endowment for the Humanities—a rare accomplishment for children's museums at that time—confirmed that the seriousness of our efforts had been recognized in more scholarly circles as well.
16. "Ironically, visitors are much more likely to utilize museums to confirm pre-existing understanding than to build new knowledge structures. However, knowing something is not the same as knowing enough. Gaps in visitors' prior knowledge can create significant barriers for learning" (Falk and Dierking 2012, 94).

Chapter 3

1. This story and several paragraphs in this chapter were originally published in Bedford 2010. Used with permission.

Chapter 4

1. The IERG website, www.ierg.net, lists numerous publications, including concrete lesson plans for using this approach in classroom teaching. A new volume, *An Imaginative Approach to Museum Education*, will join these publications in the future.
2. Creativity is much discussed in educational circles, including museums. I believe it is one possible result of engaging the imagination. In other words, imagination is necessary but not sufficient for creativity. For a discussion of the relationship of imagination as "precursor" to creativity and innovation, see Lincoln Center Institute 2011.

3. Philosophic understanding also exemplifies what Egan decries as "the lure of certainty," which he likens to the dogmatist's belief in absolute truth or the adolescent's narcissism (Egan 1997, 127–29). This can become "a narrow, disembodied rationality, which links itself with the cognitive but distances itself from the affective," a mental posture in which the imagination has "no significant role in cognition, and the emotions are considered likely only to infect it with confusion" (Egan 1997, 135–36). As philosopher Maxine Greene (2004) puts it, "ideology is the end of the imagination."
4. One of several books written for the layman on the mind-body connection, *The Body Has a Mind of Its Own,* proved an extremely readable synopsis of current research for a nonscientist like myself. Others include Johnson 1987 and Damasio 1994.

Chapter 5

1. For more about Dewey, progressive education, and Dewey's influence on museums, see Hein 2004 and Hein 2006.
2. Kenneth McClelland points out that while Dewey enjoyed museums, he also worried about how museum culture "tended to create and reinforce 'a chasm between ordinary and aesthetic experience'" (2005, 55). Dewey's enthusiasm for Albert Barnes's work at the Barnes Foundation in Philadelphia derived from, among other things, their shared commitment to education.
3. An illustration of *an* experience that, while less than life-changing, nonetheless captures Dewey's thinking, is the poem "John Dewey's Theory of Experience," by Joseph Featherstone (2007):

    The supermarket apple
    tastes like sugary wallboard,
    or pond scum in a heatwave—

    such fruit is experienced,
    then mercifully lost
    in the traffic of time.

    This wizened apple off my old tree—
    attacked every summer by cruel
    wires of bittersweet vine—
    smells of the south wind running
    across an almost-frozen harbor.

    It tastes of seasons,
    starlight, birdsong, and decay.

> The eating of it had a beginning,
> a middle, and an end.
>
> My encounter with it is an experience—
> it has made me alive again
> in every sense.

4. Dewey speaks of the continuity between art and everyday experience throughout *Art as Experience*, giving periodic examples of what he means, for example, popular music versus more "intellectual" art. He does not, according to McClelland, provide much insight into the nature of what a non-art-centered but aesthetic experience would look like (Dewey 1934 [1959] xv). It became Jackson's task to spell this out in greater detail. Therefore, much of my understanding of how this continuum would work comes from Jackson and not directly from Dewey.
5. There is no intention here to criticize either school of thought. They both provide insights into museum work, offer principles for improving it, and should be part of any practitioner's library.
6. As Egan admits in his definition of imagination, some people have more imagination than others. Here is a wonderful example of someone with a great deal of imagination who, perhaps not surprisingly, grew up to be a museum director.

   > And then when I was in fourth grade my fourth grade teacher, Mrs. Nichols, took us on a field trip to (Letchworth) Park to see the home of Mary Jamison, who was a young girl who had been taken captive by the Iroquois Indians, and she had spent the rest of her life actually married to an Iroquois Indian and set up her home in (Letchworth) Park. And so there was a cabin where she had lived. And I had a fantasy from then on that I always wanted to be Mary Jamison and be kidnapped by the Iroquois Indians and taken away into a whole new lifestyle. And I always used to fantasize what it was like to grind corn and do all those things that Mary had to do (M. Spock 1992, 5.13; 2000b, 28).

7. For a recent analysis of gallery teaching in art museums with a Deweyian-Greene perspective, see Burnham and Kai-Kee 2011.
8. Lincoln Center Institute 2007, 4–5. See also the work by Project Zero at Harvard University, including Lois Hetland and Ellen Winner's project, Teaching and Learning in the Visual Arts.
9. Certainly Dewey greatly influenced the way Albert Barnes created exhibitions of artworks at his own institution, where the focus was on educational experience throughout. See Hein 2012.

Chapter 6

1. For years I shared the scorn many of my colleagues in children's and other visitor-centered institutions had for traditional art museums, which in our view cared only for the art and the scholarship. Certainly there remain major, sometimes irreconcilable, differences in how various kinds of institutions think about mission, audience, and organizational roles. But as I have learned— often from my Bank Street students who came from art museums— art museums can be among the most progressive institutions in their communities: the Walters Art Museum, Milwaukee Art Museum, Detroit Institute of Arts, Columbus Museum of Art, Denver Art Museum, Art Gallery of Ontario, Oakland Museum of California, and others. These places not only use visitor research in designing exhibitions but also have found new ways for content and audience advocates to collaborate on exhibitions and programs. For some recent examples, see Samis and Michaelson 2013.
2. In addition to McKenna-Cress and Kamien, see Kathleen McLean's classic *Planning for People in Exhibitions* (1993).
3. Elaine Heumann Gurian (2006b) uses different language to say something very similar. She concludes that what matters is not the object but the story; museums are about stories.
4. A colleague whose field is interpretation and visitor studies joined a panel called "Metaphorically Speaking" that I organized in 2006. Coming from an art museum where the staff had often resisted efforts to translate art-talk into language that everyone could understand, he initially resisted my enthusiasm for the concept of metaphor until he saw the images I presented and understood that the point was communication with *everyone*. His response confirmed my dawning conviction that art and aesthetic experience have been allowed too often to sit on high with the masterworks and the art historical and not down among the everyday.
5. It should be noted that the term *metaphor* is used throughout this discussion similarly to the way Egan uses it—as a cognitive tool to talk about something in terms derived from something very different—rather than as it is more precisely defined in literary theory. Thus, the examples cited in this book—Wilson's shackles, the shoes in the United States Holocaust Memorial Museum, the suitcases in *Lost Cases, Recovered Lives*—function for the visitor as metaphors. They draw parallels to something different, and in so doing, open up—rather than shut down—the visitor's imagination. But they are not metaphors in the literary sense; for instance, the shoes might be more accurately termed synecdoche.
6. *Mining the Museum* was not only popular with the thousands of museum professionals who visited during the annual American Association of Museums meeting

in Baltimore that year, but also with lay visitors, including schoolchildren, who may not have grasped the irony or deeper historical significance of many of the displays but who nevertheless felt their power. See Korn and Ades 1995.

7. The reader may well wonder why this image is not included; copyright issues precluded its inclusion. I regret that other equally pertinent images were not available for this and similar reasons. I hope the reader will use his imagination.

8. Dewey was not an artist, and it is questionable how many artists would accept this statement. One who might is Olafur Eliasson, creator of *The Weather Project* at Tate Modern and many other public art installations. He remarked in an interview with staff at the San Francisco Museum of Modern Art on the importance of audience in contemporary art: "The very basic belief that is behind my work is that objecthood, or objects as such, doesn't have a place in the world if there is not an individual person making some use of that object." http://www.sfmoma.org/explore/multimedia/videos/582?autoplay=true

9. There is something about leaving an object or site in its original state that enhances its dramatic power. I assume this is because it reveals the human hand and mind at work. I am reminded of handprints on Neolithic caves or the doodles left inside Ellis Island's great hall or the grooves in the floorboards at Eldridge Street Synagogue mentioned later in this chapter.

10. See Vogler 1985; see also O'Neill 2007. For an intriguing example of how Jungian archetypes function across cultures, see Chinen 1993.

11. I am indebted to Lauri Halderman for pointing out the existence of the new field of neuroaesthetics as well as for clarifying the work of mirror neurons. As a novice, I look forward to learning over the next few years how this research can be used in the creation of exhibitions and programs. A small but noticeable number of museum professionals are in doctoral programs in cognitive science, which can only improve our practice. In addition to the Paul article, see Emory University study of metaphors involving textures, http://news.emory.edu/stories/2012/02/metaphor_brain_imaging.

12. One example among many comes from the Cleveland Museum of Art's Gallery One, also by Local Projects. Visitors can browse the entire collection in various ways, including by emotion. You make a face—happy, surprised, afraid—and the system brings up works of art that express those feelings.

13. This does not mean visitors do not read labels. They do. As Falk and Dierking note, "all visitors read some labels; no visitor reads all of them" (116). They review the significant body of research about label writing, pointing out that while "visitors will read supporting interpretive materials, . . . they are particularly attentive

to the objects and to opportunities to interact" (113). My supporting point is that we privilege reading and sight at the expense of our other senses.

14. The stories about childhood encounters with the walkthrough heart at the Franklin Institute recall Greenblatt's (see chapter 2) and Egan's (see chapter 4) definitions of wonder, that initial encounter that can lead to a lifetime of discovery. Many of these strategies apply to programs as well as exhibitions. For example, a personal favorite experience comes from the tours at the Lower East Side Tenement Museum in New York. The educators describe the challenges building residents faced as they navigated the steep stairs in long skirts, loaded down with coal, groceries, washing, and small children. Then they turn off the hall lights and the visitor is plunged into the darkness these immigrants would have known every day. It is a powerful somatic experience.
15. For a detailed discussion of the theory, process, and significance to the field of exhibition design behind the creation of the soundscape at the Pequot Museum, see Quin 1999.
16. Unfortunately, the day I visited, the effect of this understated and artful piece of theater was totally undermined by the lengthy and utterly didactic lecture of the resident park ranger.
17. There can be practical considerations: smells can be manufactured, but they fade over time and are problematic to maintain. As McKenna-Cress and Kamien point out, "artful balance in the delivery must be considered so as to not overwhelm visitors with too much of a good thing" (2013, 158). One effective example is in the *Old World—New World* exhibition at the Royal Museum of British Columbia. As you exit a replica of a 1798 square-rigged ship, the smell of tar and salt air fill your lungs and you hear the crash of waves against the hull and the sound of seagulls (Suzanne Morris, personal communication).
18. For a quick exploration of smell's impact on memory, see Tom Stafford, "Why Can Smells Unlock Forgotten Memories? *BBC Future,* March 13, 2012, *www.bbc.com/future/story/20120312-why-can-smells-unlock-memories* (accessed October 24, 2013).
19. The wands, of course, are extensions of the visitor's peripersonal space (see the discussion of embodied imagination in chapter 4).
20. As noted earlier, while most museum studies and museum education programs include at least one course on exhibitions, only a handful of places in the United States offer degrees in exhibition design. According to Jim Volkert, some thirty years ago when NAME, the professional network on exhibit development and design of the American Alliance of Museums, was founded, there was a singular lack of interest in creating any kind of professional licensing or certification pro-

gram for designers who considered the variety of backgrounds they brought to the work a source of its excellence. See NAME 2006 for a discussion of the pros and cons of classroom training in exhibit design.

21. Peter Samis, curator of interpretation at the San Francisco Museum of Modern Art, questions the extent to which most artists are concerned with the general viewer's aesthetic experience. While most artists do have viewers in mind, he suggests those viewers are more often artist peers, critics, or curators. The artists work first for themselves and second for someone who might recognize the problem they are attempting to solve and their ingenuity in solving it. Samis is also the colleague who introduced me to artist Olafur Eliasson's commitment to public engagement with his works (see n. 66), so generalizations are difficult. He notes that Marcel Duchamp, progenitor of conceptual art, also insisted that the viewer completes the work of art.

22. Anyone looking to grasp the potential of new technologies for museums can peruse the *NMC Horizon Report: Museum Edition* (www.nmc.org/horizon-project/horizon-reports/horizon-report-museum-edition) as well as the Center for the Future of Museums blog from the American Alliance of Museums (http://futureofmuseums.blogspot.com). Social media, 3-D printing, natural user interfaces, augmented reality, and game-based learning are only a few of the tools currently available or on the horizon for museum implementation.

23. This scholarly work grew out of a conference hosted by the Universities of Leicester and Nottingham in 2010. According to the editors, it speaks to "a vision of the museum as theatre, as dramatic ritual, as a telling of the world in miniature, and as a site where space and place making connect with human perception, imagination and memory" (Macleod et al. 2012, xxi). It includes chapters on scenic design, embodied imagination, and many of the themes addressed here.

24. Visit the International Museum Theatre Alliance website, imtal.org, for further information. The longitudinal study is available at: www.plh.manchester.ac.uk (accessed October 24, 2013). Indiana's Conner Prairie has pioneered the design of highly immersive theatrical experiences such as *Follow the North Star,* where participants become runaway slaves on the Underground Railroad, a journey across the history park's landscape at night that delivers a powerful emotional punch.

25. There are other effective ways of constructing a narrative while honoring the visitor's desire to follow her own path. For example, within the overarching narrative of the *Darwin* exhibition were several sections, each with its own narrative, a technique also evident in *Open House* and *Noah's Ark*.

Conclusion

1. Charles Isherwood, "Stories that Tell vs. Storytelling," *New York Times,* May 6, 2005, www.nytimes.com/2005/05/06/theater/newsandfeatures/06note.html?_r=0 (accessed October 24, 2013).
2. David Comer Kidd and Emanuele Castano, "Reading Literary Fiction Improves Theory of Mind," *Science* 342, no. 6156 (October 18, 2013), www.sciencemag.org/content/342/6156/377.abstract, (accessed October 24, 2013); Pam Belluck, "For Better Social Skills, Scientists Recommend a Little Chekhov," *New York Times,* October 3. 2013, http://well.blogs.nytimes.com/2013/10/03/i-know-how-youre-feeling-i-read-chekhov (accessed October 24, 2013).
3. O'Neill's analysis of terror management theory with regard to museum practice notes that a culturally comparative approach to museum displays, conventionally assumed to promote mutual understanding and tolerance, may in truth do just the opposite (2012, 67–69).

References

Abbott, H. Porter. 2002. *The Cambridge Introduction to Narrative*. Cambridge: Cambridge University Press.

Ackerman, Diane. 1994. *A Natural History of Love*. New York: Random House.

Anderson, Gail, ed. 2012. *Reinventing the Museum: The Evolving Conversation on the Paradigm Shift*. 2nd ed. Lanham, Md.: AltaMira Press.

Barton, Jake. 2013. "The Museum of You." TED Talk. http://www.ted.com/talks/jake_barton_the_museum_of_you.html (accessed October 25, 2013).

Bedford, Leslie. 2001. "Storytelling: The Real Work of Museums." *Curator: The Museum Journal* 44 (1): 27–34.

———. 2005. "Lost Cases: Recovered Lives." *Curator: The Museum Journal* 48 (2): 213–20.

———. 2008. "Noah's Ark at the Skirball Cultural Center" (exhibition review). *Informal Learning Review*, January/February, 12–14.

———. 2010. "Finding the Story in History." In *Connecting Kids to History with Museum Exhibitions*, edited by D. Lynn McRainey and John Russick, 97–116. Walnut Creek, Calif.: Left Coast Press.

———. 2012. "Musing about Time and Museums." *Curator: The Museum Journal* 55 (4): 393–400.

Blakeslee, Sandra, and Matthew Blakeslee. 2007. *The Body Has a Mind of Its Own*. New York: Random House.

Boston Children's Museum. 2013. *Boston Stories: The Children's Museum as a Model for Nonprofit Leadership*. Michael Spock, project director. Edited by Mary Maher.

Boyd, Brian. 2009. *On the Origin of Stories: Evolution, Cognition, and Fiction*. Cambridge, Mass.: Belknap Press, Harvard University.

Braden, Donna, Ellen Rosenthal, and Daniel Spock. 2005. "What the Heck Is Experience Design?" *The Exhibitionist* 24 (2): 14–20.

Bruner, Jerome. 1986. *Actual Minds, Possible Worlds*. Cambridge, Mass.: Harvard University Press.

———. 1990. *Acts of Meaning: The Jerusalem-Harvard Lectures*. Cambridge, Mass: Harvard University Press.

Burnham, Rika, and Elliott Kai-Kee. 2011. *Teaching in the Art Museum: Interpretation as Experience*. Los Angeles: Getty Publications.

Chinen, Allan B. 1993. *Once Upon a Midlife: Classic Stories and Mythic Tales to Illuminate the Middle Years*. New York: Putnam.

Chodakowski, Anne, and Kieran Egan. "The Body's Role in Our Intellectual Education." Imaginative Education Research Group. http://ierg.net/assets/documents/publications/IERGBodyrole.pdf (accessed October 25, 2013).

Conn, Steven. 1998. *Museums and American Intellectual Life: 1876–1926*. Chicago: University of Chicago Press.

Connolly, Geraldine. 1998. "The Summer I Was Sixteen." In *Province of Fire*. Oakridge, Tenn.: Iris.

Corrin, Lisa G. 1994. "Mining the Museum: Artists Look at Museums, Museums Look at Themselves." In *Mining the Museum: An Installation*, edited by Lisa G. Corrin, 1–22. New York: New Press.

Crew, Spencer, and James E. Sims. 1991. "Locating Authenticity: Fragments of a Dialogue." In *Exhibiting Cultures: The Poetics and Politics of Museum Display*, edited by Ivan Karp and Stephen D. Lavine, 159–75. Washington, D.C.: Smithsonian Institution Press.

Csikszentmihalyi, Mihaly. 1997. "Assessing Aesthetic Education: Measuring the Ability to 'Ward Off Chaos.'" *Grantmakers in the Arts* 8 (1): 22–26.

———, and Rick E. Robinson. 1990. *The Art of Seeing: An Interpretation of the Aesthetic Encounter*. Malibu, Calif.: J. Paul Getty Trust.

Cutler, Anna. 2012. "What Is to Be Done, Sandra? Learning in Cultural Institutions of the 21st Century." In *Reinventing the Museum: The Evolving Conversation on the Paradigm Shift*, 2nd ed., edited by Gail Anderson, 351–63. Lanham, Md., AltaMira Press.

Damasio, Antonio R. 1994. *Descartes's Error: Emotion, Reason, and the Human Brain*. New York: Putnam.

Dewey, John. 1934 [1959]. *Art as Experience*. Reprint, New York: Capricorn.

———. 1923. Letter 17469. June 15, 1923. Unpublished correspondence of John Dewey, Center for John Dewey Studies, Southern Illinois University, Carbondale.

———. 1938. *Experience and Education*. Reprint, West Lafayette, Ind.: Kappa Delta Pi, 1998.

———. 2008. "The Philosophy of the Arts." In *John Dewey: The Later Works, 1925–1953*, edited by Jo Ann Boydston, vol. 13, 357–68. Carbondale: Southern Illinois University Press.

Egan, Kieran. 1983. "Accumulating History." In *The Philosophy of History Teaching*. Middletown, Conn.: Wesleyan University Press, 66–80.

———. 1985. "Imagination and Learning." *Teachers College Record* 87 (2): 155–71.

———. 1989. *Teaching as Story Telling: An Alternative Approach to Teaching and Curriculum in the Elementary School*. Chicago: University of Chicago Press.

———. 1997. *The Educated Mind: How Cognitive Tools Shape Our Understanding*. Chicago: University of Chicago Press.

———. 2003. "Start with What the Student Knows or with What the Student Can Imagine?" *Phi Delta Kappan* (February): 443–45.

———. 2005. "Somatic Understanding: The Body's Toolkit." E-mail to the author, April 1.

———. 2008. "Culture and Education: The Omitted Chapter, Part One." http://www.educ.sfu.ca/kegan/omitted.html (accessed October 25, 2013).

———. 2007. "A Very Short History of the Imagination." www.mantleofthe expert.com/studying/articles/KE%20-%20History%20of%20Imagination.pdf.

Egan, Kieran, and Dan Nadaner, eds. 1988. *Imagination and Education*. New York: Teachers College Press.

Ellenbogen, Kirsten, Beth Janetski, and Murphy Pizza. 2006a. "Open House: If These Walls Could Talk." Summative evaluation report. Science Museum of Minnesota Department of Evaluation and Research in Learning, St. Paul.

———. 2006b. "Appendix: Open House Transcripts." Science Museum of Minnesota Department of Evaluation and Research in Learning, St. Paul.

Erskine-Loftus, Pamela, ed. 2013. *Reimagining Museums: Practice in the Arabian Peninsula*. Edinburgh and Boston: MuseumsEtc.

National Association for Museum Exhibition (NAME). 2006. *The Exhibitionist* 25, no. 1 (25th anniversary issue). http://name-aam.org/uploads/downloadables/16119_NAME_spg06_lores.pdf (accessed October 24, 2013).

Falk, John H. 2006. "An Identity-Centered Approach to Understanding Museum Learning." *Curator: The Museum Journal* 49 (2): 151–66.

Falk, John H., and Lynn D. Dierking. *The Museum Experience*. 1992. Washington, D.C.: Whalesback Books, 1992.

———. 2000. *Learning from Museums: Visitor Experiences and the Making of Meaning*. Walnut Creek, Calif.: AltaMira Press.

———. 2013. *The Museum Experience Revisited*. Walnut Creek, Calif.: Left Coast Press.

Featherstone, Joseph. 2007. "John Dewey's Theory of Experience." Unpublished poem, in e-mail to the author, October 7.

Frye, Northrop. 1964. *The Educated Imagination*. Bloomington: Indiana University Press.

Garcia, Ben, ed. 2010. *Journal of Museum Education*. 2010. *Museum Education and Public Value. Journal of Museum Education* 35, no. 1 (Spring).

Garcia, Ben. 2012. "What We Do Best: Making the Case for Museum Learning in Its Own Right." *Journal of Museum Education* 37 (2): 47–56.

Greenblatt, Stephen. 1991. "Resonance and Wonder." In *Exhibiting Cultures: The Poetics and Politics of Museum Display*, edited by Ivan Karp and Stephen D. Lavine, 42–56. Washington, D.C.: Smithsonian Books.

Greene, Maxine. 1985. "Imagination and Learning: A Reply to Kieran Egan." *Teachers College Record* 87 (2): 155–71.

———. 1988. "What Happened to Imagination?" In *Imagination and Education,* edited by Kieran Egan and Dan Nadaner. New York: Teachers College Press, 45–56.

———. 2001. *Variations on a Blue Guitar: The Lincoln Center Institute Lectures on Aesthetic Education*. New York: Teachers College Press.

———. 2004. Faculty Seminar on Aesthetic Education. Bank Street College of Education, New York, November 19.

Gurian, Elaine Heumann. 2000. Interview with the author. March 1.

———. 2006a. *Civilizing the Museum: The Collected Writings of Elaine Heumann Gurian*. New York: Routledge.

———. 2006b. "What is the Object of This Exercise?" In *Civilizing the Museum: The Collected Writings of Elaine Heumann Gurian*. New York: Routledge. 33–47.

———. 2011. "Wanting to Be the Third on the Block." http://www.egurian.com/omnium-gatherum/museum-issues/leadership/directors-issues/wanting-to-be-the-third-on-your-block (accessed October 28, 2013).

Hein, George. 1998. *Learning in the Museum*. London: Routledge.

———. 1999. "Is Meaning Making Constructivism? Is Constructivism Meaning Making?" *The Exhibitionist* 18 (2): 15–18.

———. 2004. "John Dewey and Museum Education." *Curator: The Museum Journal* 47 (4): 413–27.

———. 2006a. "John Dewey's Wholly Original Philosophy and Its Significance for Museums." *Curator: The Museum Journal* 49 (2): 181–203.

———. 2006b. "Museum Education." In *A Companion to Museum Studies,* edited by S. MacDonald, chapter 20. Oxford: Blackwell Publishing.

———. 2012. *Progressive Museum Practice: John Dewey and Democracy*. Walnut Creek, Calif.: Left Coast Press.

Hooper-Greenhill, Eilean. 1992. *Museums and the Shaping of Knowledge*. London: Routledge.

Husbands, Chris. 1996. *What is History Teaching? Language, Ideas, and Meaning in Learning about the Past*. Buckingham, Pa.: Open University Press.

Imaginative Education Research Group. 2013. "A Brief Guide to Imaginative Education." http://ierg.net/about/briefguide.html (accessed October 24, 2013).

Isherwood, Charles. 2005. "Critic's Notebook: Stories That Tell vs. Storytelling." *New York Times*, May 6, 2005, E1.

Jackson, Philip W. 1998. *John Dewey and the Lessons of Art*. New Haven: Yale University Press.

Johnson, Mark L. 1987. *The Body in the Mind: The Bodily Basis of Meaning, Imagination, and Reason*. Chicago: University of Chicago Press.

———. 2004. *Mind Wide Open: Your Brain and the Neuroscience of Everyday Life*. New York: Scribner's.

Jones, Mike. 2012. "On Storyworlds, Immersive Media, Narrative, and Museums." Interview by Seb Chan, in *Fresh & New(er)*, October 2. http://www.freshandnew.org/2012/10/storyworlds-immersive-media-narrative-interview-mike-jones/ (accessed October 28, 2013).

Kaplan, Abraham. 1981. "Introduction to *Art as Experience*." In *John Dewey: The Later Works, 1925–1953*, edited by Jo Ann Boydston, vol. 10, vii–xxxiii. Carbondale: Southern Illinois University Press.

Keillor, Garrison. 2000. "In Search of Lake Wobegon." *National Geographic* 198 (6): 87–109.

Korn, Randi, and Susan Ades. 1995. "An Evaluation of the *Mining the Museum* Museum/School Partnership Program." Unpublished research report. Alexandria, Va.: Randi Korn & Associates.

Kulik, Gary. 1992. "Introduction." In *Mermaids, Mummies, and Mastodons: The Emergence of the American Museum*, edited by William T. Alderson. Washington, D.C.: American Association of Museums.

Latham, Kiersten F. 2007. "The Poetry of the Museum: A Holistic Model of Numinous Museum Experiences." *Museum Management and Curatorship* 22 (3): 247–63.

———. 2013a. "Numinous Experiences With Museum Objects." *Visitor Studies* 16 (1): 3–20.

———. 2013b. "What is the Real Thing in the Museum?" http://prezi.com/fhorvgm6esgj/what-is-the-real-thing-in-the-museum (accessed October 24, 2013).

Leinhardt, Gaea, Carol Tittle, and Karen Knudson. 2002. "Talking to Oneself: Diaries of Museum Visits." In *Learning Conversations in Museums*, edited by Gaea Leinhardt, Kevin Crowley, and Karen Knutson, 103–33. Mahwah, N.J.: Lawrence Erlbaum.

Lincoln Center Institute. 2007. *Aesthetic Education, Inquiry, and the Imagination*.

———. 2011. "Learning to Imagine." www.lcinstitute.org/component/docman/cat_view/88-reports-a-resources (accessed October 24, 2013).

Luke, Jessica J., and Marianna Adams. 2008. "What Research Says About Learning in Art Museums." In *From Periphery to Center: Art Museum Education in the 21st Century*, edited by P. Vileneuve. Reston, Va.: National Art Education Association.

Luke, Jessica J., and Karen Knutson. 2010. "Beyond Science: Implications of the *LSIE* Report for Art Museum Education." *Curator: The Museum Journal* 53 (2): 229–37.

Macleod, Suzanne, Laura Hourston Hanks, and Jonathan Hale, eds. 2012. *Museum Making: Narratives, Architectures, Exhibitions*. London: Routledge.

McClelland, Kenneth A. 2005. "John Dewey: Aesthetic Experience and Artful Conduct." *Education and Culture: The Journal of the John Dewey Society* 21 (2): 41–62.

McKenna-Cress, Polly, and Janet A. Kamien. 2013. *Creating Exhibitions: Collaboration in the Planning, Development, and Design of Innovative Experiences.* Hoboken, N.J.: John Wiley and Sons.

McLean, Kathleen. 1993. *Planning for People in Exhibitions*. Washington, D.C.: Association of Science-Technology Centers.

———. 1999. "Museum Exhibitions and the Dynamics of Dialogue." *Daedalus* 128 (3): 83–108.

McMahan, Alison. 2003. "Immersion, Engagement, and Presence: A Method for Analyzing 3-D Video Games." In *The Video Game Theory Reader*, edited by Mark Wolf and Bernard Perron, 67–86. New York: Routledge.

Merriell, Andrew. 2005. Interview with the author. January 21.

Minnesota Historical Society. 2003. "Revised Preliminary Development Sign-Off Document" (internal communication). St. Paul, May 15.

Moore, Mark H. 1997. *Creating Public Value: Strategic Management in Government*. Cambridge, Mass.: Harvard University Press.

Museums Association. 2013. "Conference Themes: The Emotional Museum." http://www.museumsassociation.org/conference/05062013-conference-2013-themes (accessed October 28, 2013).

O'Neill, Mark. 2007. "Kelvingrove: Telling Stories in a Treasured Old/New Museum." *Curator: The Museum Journal* 50 (4): 379–97.

———. 2010. "Cultural Attendance and Public Mental Health: From Research to Practice." *Journal of Public Mental Health* 9 (4): 22–29.

———. 2012. "Museums and Mortality." *Material Religion: The Journal of Objects, Art and Belief* 8 (1): 52–75.

Ott, Maureen. 2001. "What is Interpretation? Unpublished Notes From a Talk to the Board of the Minnesota History Center." Letter to author, June 3.

Paul, Annie Murphy. 2012. Your Brain on Fiction. *New York Times*, March 18. http://www.nytimes.com/2012/03/18/opinion/sunday/the-neuroscience-of-your-brain-on-fiction.html?_r=1&pagewanted=all (accessed October 28, 2013).

Polland, Annie. 2009. *Landmark of the Spirit: The Eldridge Street Synagogue*. New Haven: Yale University Press.

Quin, Douglas Hyder. 1999. "Nature by Design: Soundscape in the Museum." Ph.D. dissertation, Union Institute and University.

Rand, Judy. 2010. "Write and Design with the Family in Mind." In *Connecting Kids to History through Exhibitions*, edited by D. Lynn McRainey and John Russick, 257–84. Walnut Creek, Calif.: Left Coast Press.

Roberts, Lisa C. 1997. *From Knowledge to Narrative: Educators and the Changing Museum*. Washington, D.C.: Smithsonian Institution Press.

Rossiter, Marsha. 1999. "Understanding Adult Development as Narrative." *New Directions in Adult and Continuing Education* 84: 77–85.

———. 2002. "Narrative and Stories in Adult Teaching and Learning." *ERIC Digest* 241. ED473147. http://eric.ed.gov/?q=marsha+rossiter&id=ED473147 (accessed October 28, 2013).

Rounds, Jay. 2004. "Strategies for the Curiosity-Driven Museum Visitor." *Curator: The Museum Journal* 47 (4): 389–412.

———. 2006. "Doing Identity Work in Museums." *Curator: The Museum Journal* 49 (2): 133–50.

Samis, Peter, and Mimi Michaelson. 2013. "Meaning-Making in Nine Acts." *The Exhibitionist,* Spring 2013, 54–59. http://name-aam.org/uploads/downloadables/EXH.spr_13/12%20EXH_SP13_Meaning%20Making%20in%20Nine%20Acts_Samis_Michaelson.pdf (accessed October 28, 2013).

Schwartzer, Marjorie. 2004. "The Exhibition: From Cases to Spaces." Unpublished draft.

———. 2006. *Riches, Rivals and Radicals: 100 Years of Museums in America*. Washington, D.C.: American Association of Museums.

Scott, Carol, ed. 2013. *Museums and Public Value: Creating Sustainable Futures.* London: Ashgate.

Shettel, Harris H. 1973. "Exhibits: Art Form or Educational Medium?" *Museum News* 52 (9): 32–41.

Silverman, Lois. 1991. *Of Us and Other "Things": The Content and Function of Talk by Adult Visitor Pairs in an Art and a History Museum*. Ph.D. dissertation, Indiana University.

———. 1993. "Making Meaning Together: Lessons from the Field of American History." *Journal of Museum Education* 18 (3): 7–11.

———. 1995. "Visitor Meaning-Making in Museums for a New Age." *Curator: The Museum Journal* 38 (3): 161–70.

———. 2002. "Taking a Wider View of Museum Outcomes and Experiences: Theory, Research, and Magic." *Journal of Education in Museums* 23: 3–8.

———. 2010. *The Social Work of Museums*. New York and Oxford: Routledge.

Simon, Nina. 2010. *The Participatory Museum*. http://www.participatorymuseum.org (accessed October 28, 2013).

———. 2011. "Participatory Design and the Future of Museums." In *Letting Go? Sharing Historical Authority in a User-Generated World,* edited by Bill Adair, Benjamin Filene, and Laura Koloski. Philadelphia: Pew Center for Arts and Heritage/Left Coast Press.

Spence, David, Tom Wareham, Caroline Bressey, June Bam-Hutchinson, and Annette Day. 2013. "The Public as Co-Producers: Making the *London, Sugar, and Slave Gallery*, Museum of London Docklands." In Carol Scott, ed., *Museums and Public Value: Creating Sustainable Futures.* London: Ashgate, 99–109.

Spock, Daniel. 2004. "Is it Interactive Yet?" *Curator: The Museum Journal* 47 (4): 369–74.

———. 2006a. Lincolns in Latex. *Curator: The Museum Journal* 49 (1): 95–104.

———. 2006b. "The Puzzle of Museum Educational Practice: A Comment on Rounds and Falk." *Curator: The Museum Journal* 49 (2): 167–80.

———. 2007. "Personal Connections." PowerPoint presentation, American Association for State and Local History, Atlanta, September 5–8.

Spock, Michael. 1992. "Philadelphia Stories: A Collection of 75 Transcripts." Unpublished transcripts, 1992.

———. 1999a. "Elegant Programs and Conversations." In *Presence of Mind: Museums and the Spirit of Learning,* edited by Bonnie Pitman-Gelles, 141–49. Washington, D.C.: American Association of Museums.

———. 1999b. "The Stories We Tell about Meaning Making." *The Exhibitionist* 18 (2); 30–34.

———. 2000a. "Listening to Stories We Tell about Troubled Kids and Children's Museums: Ambivalence about Our Therapeutic Role." *Hand to Hand* 14 (4): 1–2, 6.

———, ed. 2000b. *A Study Guide to Philadelphia Stories: A Collection of Pivotal Museum Memories.* Washington, D.C.: American Association of Museums.

———. 2000c. "Tales of Alonetime and Owntime in Museums." *Journal of Museum Education* 25 (1): 15–19.

———. 2000c. "When I Grow Up I Want to Work in a Place Like This." *Curator: The Museum Journal* 41 (1): 19–30.

Spock, Michael, and Hope J. Leichter. 1999. "Learning From Ourselves: Pivotal Stories of Museum Professionals." In *Bridges to Understanding Children's Museums*, edited by Nina Freedlander Gibans and Barbara Kres Beach, 41–81. Cleveland: Case Western Reserve University.

Steiner, Wendy. 2004. "Pictorial Narrativity." In *Narrative Across Media: The Languages of Storytelling*, edited by Marie-Laure Ryan, 145–77. Lincoln: University of Nebraska Press.

Sullivan, Graeme. 2006. "Aesthetic Education at Lincoln Center Institute: An Historical and Philosophic Overview." March 12. [*Ed. Note:* Online document; URL has expired.]

Sutton-Smith, Brian. 1988. "In Search of the Imagination." In *Imagination and Education*, edited by Egan Kieran and Dan Nadaner, 3–29. New York: Teachers College Press.

Tencer, Golda. 1996. *And I Still See Their Faces: Images of Polish Jews.* Warsaw: Amerykan sko-Polsko-Izraelska Fundacja "Shalom."

Tilden, Freeman. 1957. *Interpreting Our Heritage: Principles and Practices for Visitor Services in Parks, Museums, and Historic Places.* Chapel Hill: University of North Carolina Press.

Toumani, Meline. 2005. "Graduating From High School for Their Annual King Day Show." *New York Times*, January 15, B9.

Volkert, James. 2005. Interview with the author. January 23.

———. 2006. "On the Occasion of Tut's Return." *The Exhibitionist* 25 (1): 40–42.

Vogler, Christopher. 1985. "A Practical Guide to Joseph Campbell's *The Hero with a Thousand Faces*." http://www.thewritersjourney.com/hero%27s_journey.htm (accessed October 28, 2013).

Weil, Stephen E. 1999. "From Being *about* Something to Being *for* Somebody: The Ongoing Transformation of the American Museum." *Daedalus* 128 (3): 229–55.

Index

Note: Italicized page numbers indicate illustrations.

ABOUT THE AUTHOR

Leslie Bedford is an independent consultant, the former director of the Leadership in Museum Education program of the Bank Street Graduate School of Educationprogram, and a member of The Museum Group. She holds a Ph.D. in museum studies from Union Institute & University and a master's degree in education from Harvard University. Bedford previously worked at the Brooklyn Historical Society and the Boston Children's Museum. Her writings have appeared in *Curator: The Museum Journal*, *Exhibitionist*, and other key museum publications.